New Life in Country Music

To Tony & Ann
with Christian Greetings

Paul Davis

Romans 8: 28-29

PTL!

New Life in Country Music

BY

PAUL DAVIS

with:

Foreword by CLIFF RICHARD

and Introduction by GEORGE HAMILTON IV

Illustrations by RICHARD DEVERELL

Henry Walter Ltd.
Worthing, Sussex.

ISBN 085479 591 X

© Paul Davis 1976

Published by
Henry E. Walter Ltd.
26 Grafton Rd., Worthing, Sussex.

Printed in Great Britain by
Tonbridge Printers Ltd., Peach Hall Works,
Tonbridge, Kent

Contents

Introduction

Someone has said, 'The greatest sermon of all is a life well lived.' That's what this book is all about – the personal testimonies and witnesses and life stories of some friends of mine and some folks I don't even know, but *wish* I did. Many of the country music artists featured in this book have had a profound influence on me and how I view life and it's meaning – I'm grateful to my dear friend Paul Davis for giving me the opportunity to say a word or two here. Paul is a good man and a true believer, and I hope someday I can be *one tenth* the person he thinks I am! It's the love and goodness of Paul and our friends he has written about that make me want to try harder and better to *BE* what I believe!

Thanks, Paul, for a beautiful book and for your beautiful life.

Your friend

GEORGE HAMILTON IV

Dedicated to:

MY DEAR WIFE – HAZEL;

OUR WONDERFUL CHILDREN – ANITA AND WESLEY;

OUR FAITHFUL PARENTS – MR. AND MRS. TOM DAVIS AND MR. AND MRS. WALTER SCOTT;

OUR LOVING CHURCH – IN GROVE PARK AND WORLDWIDE;

ALL OUR FRIENDS – IN 'THE WORLD OF COUNTRY MUSIC'.

Foreword

I don't know anyone else with as much knowledge of country music as Paul Davis. From personal experience I've discovered him to be a total source of information!

During preparation for my Sunday morning 'Gospel Road' radio series, I needed, very naturally, a reliable pool of Gospel music and as most country singers are into Gospel songs (regardless of their own convictions), P.D. was a natural choice as programme researcher. Well, I've no idea what his general knowledge is like – but if 'country' was his specialist subject, we'd have a new 'mastermind'! I relied absolutely on Paul for the bits of information I fed to my listeners about the artists whose records I played. I'm sure it's his love for the music that makes him so obviously interested in the singers as people.

The artists he has featured in this book are all well known and respected exponents of country and western music. And to discover that their Gospel music stems from their personal Christian commitment is to me a bonus when it comes to my enjoying their work.

I'm sure Paul will have to compile yet another set of 'dossiers' on the many artists he knows so much about. Meanwhile, here in this book are thirteen 'insights' to be getting on with. I hope you enjoy it as much as I did!

Sincerely,

CLIFF RICHARD.

Prologue

In the early pioneering days of the New World an individual's faith grew strong under the pressures and strains of hardship and privation. History records the debt Americans owe to the Christian Faith for the supply of strength, comfort, assurance and a purpose for existence in the face of heart-breaking disappointment and struggle.

How the pioneers would love to gather in those old-fashioned days for tent-meetings, and 'all-day-sings' – often with 'dinner-on-the-ground'. Or, even around the cosy fireside with friends and loved ones on cold, winter nights for a family sing-a-long. And in the summer on the veranda of the log cabin, or a white-washed cottage, the event was repeated hundreds of times to the background accompaniment of crickets and songbirds also enjoying the cool of the evening.

The pioneers who settled the 13 original States, and who later migrated further westward, sang their songs to the accompaniment of stringed instruments. The hardships endured by them were made more bearable by their songs of inspiration and their faith in the teachings of Christianity. This faith was expressed by preachers and the congregations in small rural churches throughout the growing United States.

Where churches were not available, itinerant ministers carried the Gospel into the backwoods and hills. Calls to worship nearly always meant joining together in singing the Gospel. Musical accompaniment was generally quite simple . . . real, country harmony singing backed by the traditional string instruments particularly the 5 string banjo. And when you add to that a down-to-earth sincerity and identification with the sentiments of the songs – then the beauty of the message penetrates the consciousness of every listener. (Just a side-line: the banjo is reputed to be the only instrument to have originated in America . . . handed down from the traditions of the Eastern mountain states.)

The instruments used in Gospel music were almost identical to those used in American country music so it was only natural that country music artists learned these songs during their 'growin'-up time' and included a large amount of gospel and sacred music as a part of their regular entertainment programmes.

Country Music and Christianity have grown up together into the contemporary US, music scene. Where the two have crossed we find a rare art form, as continuous cross-fertilization takes place. As George Hamilton IV suggests 'Country Music and Gospel Music have always been closely linked. I was born in what they call the 'Bible Belt' which is a section of the States that's *very* religiously-orientated. The area has lots of churches and most people are actively involved in church activities.'

Bill Anderson of MCA Records, another of Country Music's big time artists made this comment in conversation with Cliff Richard on the BBC Radio One and Two 'Gospel Road' show: 'The musical pattern of Gospel Music has more than a passing similarity to Country Music . . . the three chord pattern, simple, direct poetry and meaningful lyrics.'

Many of the songs have been handed down from one

generation to another by ear; father to son, mother to daughter. Untrained voices, hand-made instruments and learning to 'pick and sing' by ear are heritages common to both Country Music and Gospel Music. The American Negro who sang spirituals in the fields as he worked also made a large contribution to this music source, and many of the old spirituals were adapted by the settlers, and later by country music entertainers.

Country Music has always been in essence a 'home-grown' commodity. And yet a commercially acceptable spectator-form of the music has swept across the World to capture the attention and devotion of millions in all walks of life.

As country music became a prominent part of the American musical scene, an increasing amount of sacred and gospel music was included in the Country Stars' repertoire. The 'Grand Ole Opry' and other country music shows which have developed, through radio, and later television, added emphasis and popularity to the Country-Gospel movement. Personal appearances by country artists nearly always include gospel songs. It is the expected practice to sing Gospel songs and adhere to traditional Christian beliefs if one is a country Music entertainer. However, tradition is not always the only motivating factor as RCA's Skeeter Davis declares, 'I enjoy singing Gospel Music because I'm a Christian; so, I sing it from the *heart*. I don't just sing it to throw in a Gospel song! I *identify* with the songs I sing so I'm pretty choosey about the material – it has to mean something to me.'

Today's affluence has brought with its blessings an air of personal independence, a lack of family closeness, and, in many quarters, a rejection of the traditions, principals, and faith on which America's greatness was founded. As someone once said, 'Things ain't what they used to be!'

Many, however, *still* find peace and joy in the 'old-fashioned' faith that caused their forefathers to sing. They find this faith just as vital and necessary in their times of affluence as their predecessors did in times of privation.

I: Pat Boone—The Golden Voiced Balladeer

One of the most popular people to emerge from Nashville is the golden voiced balladeer – Pat Boone. Sad songs, happy songs, old songs, new songs . . . whatever the music, whatever the mood – the sweet romance of 'April Love' the fervent high spirits of 'A wonderful time up there', the sentimental nostalgia of 'I'll be Home', the beauty of 'Friendly Persuasion' – they all became 'hit' songs when the rich, smooth voice of Pat Boone caressed them. Every performance of the late 50's and 60's became best sellers and every popular music fan knew his special sound – the splendid combination of Pat's appealing voice and Billy Vaughn's fine orchestral backing. Pat Boone's reign of success in the pop charts of the mid 1950's through to the early 60's brought him a total of thirteen gold records and the kind of following equalled only by Elvis Presley. This 'Hit Parade' success disguised his Nashville background and affinity to Country Music which did not blossom fully until his recordings with the First Nashville Jesus Band.

Pat's success was perhaps all the more remarkable because of the unlikely mixture of rock n' roll songs and tender love songs that helped keep his popularity consistently high. He scored his first million seller with the Fats Domino classic 'Ain't that a shame', switched direction with a beautiful ballad 'I'll be Home' then

began notching up a steady chart domination with hits like 'Love letters in the Sand', 'Moody River', April Love' and then, incredibly in 1962 the gimmicky 'Speedy Gonzales' gave him yet another Gold Disc. Hit record success kept pace with film acclaim and Boone fans flocked in their thousands to see him in 'Bernadine', 'April Love' and 'State Fair'.

The descendant of American folk hero Daniel Boone, Pat had come a long way since graduation at Columbia

University and a winning spot on the Ted Mack Amateur Hour. By 1962, the year 'Speedy Gonzales' made No. 1, his popularity was at an all-time high and he boasted a steady fan following. The reason was clear: Pat had a very special way with honest, warmhearted sentiment, a way that has endeared him to the millions who watched his films and television shows and listened to his records.

In everything Pat Boone sang, a quality of a sincere belief in what he was offering asserted itself, whether it was a ballad of love or his treatment of hymns and songs of inspiration, as witnessed by the reception accorded the old albums 'Hymns we Love', 'He Leadeth me', and 'My God and I'. He is undoubtedly one of the all-time leaders in record sales. No one other than Bing Crosby has commanded the world-wide popularity with both the youth and adult audience that Pat Boone enjoyed.

Early in his career, Pat Boone became the centre of publicity and half-sarcastic attention because of his modest expression of his Faith. He had climbed to the top of the popularity charts without resorting to long hair, flashy appearance or wild behaviour. As a civil, well-groomed spokesman of youthful fervour, Boone worked attempting to underplay his devotion to preclude claims of using Faith as a 'gimmick'. Almost everywhere Pat went his public surrounded him – newsmen, photographers, agents, music publishers, and of course, a legion of admirers. Such constant attention follows inevitably when a person becomes one of the World's favourite singers.

Pat has always had strong Christian convictions. Born in Jacksonville, Florida, his family moved to Donelson just outside Nashville, Tennessee, when he was four. His earliest memories of Donelson were of sitting with the rest of his family in the front row of the local Church of Christ every Sunday.

'Sitting on the front row led to some difficulties until I was about six or seven and learned that I was supposed to sit and listen!' he recounts. 'Over and over again Mama had to take me out of the service and beat the living daylights out of me for playing around on the front seats and making faces at people. But I finally got the message that church was somehow different from a playground!'

'When I was 13 I became a Christian during a stage in my life when there was absolutely no doubt that there was a God and that he expected something of me. In my college days at Columbia University I went through the usual questioning process. You start asking yourself, 'Is it possible that I've accepted another fable like Santa Claus or the Easter Bunny, or is there really a God?' In college you're not only encouraged to think but you're exposed to a lot of scepticism, pragmatism and outright atheism; and if you don't question things you're considered pretty simple-minded.'

He reasoned things out, and left college convinced that there was, in fact a God personally interested in him. But life was not plain sailing after that and that's what his book 'A New Song' is all about. He comments, 'It's about the time when I eventually just fell off the deep end in the sixties for a period of several years. I gave up trying to live anything like the kind of life I thought God wanted me to live. I kept up the pretence and the outward appearances all the time, including going to church. But I went to Sinatra-type parties and was beginning to be included in the 'in' group associated with Dean Martin, Frank Sinatra and Sammy Davies.'

Pat's deeper commitment to the Christian faith, however, came in the sixties when the entertainment industry started to move in fresh directions.

'As I felt that I couldn't go entirely with the trends of the music because we were getting into real acid rock which was totally impossible for me, I began to wonder whether I wasn't out of step in other ways as well.'

'So, for several years, I made more and more compromises and learned that I could fit in very well in the Hollywood community – and did some things which shocked people a little bit. But, in the process, I was losing my marriage and my family . . . the classic pattern of the entertainer who rises to the top and then loses everything that's really important.'

A turning point in Pat's life was when he read 'The Cross and the Switchblade'. He was really impressed with the book and suggested to the author that someone ought to make a movie out of it. David Wilkerson informed Pat that he had been approached about it before but he was not really sure if he wanted a movie made of it because Hollywood had a way of twisting things and the finished product would probably be nothing like what actually happened. But the film was made . . .

Pat describes the book as 'a true story of a man who truly believed in miracles and staked his life on the proposition that God would perform supernatural things in the lives of those who are really committed to Him. 'When I met some other people I realized that what I needed in my life was miracles too – a family miracle and a marriage miracle'.

At about this time he reached a crisis financially. Heavy investments he had made in various companies had been lost through one disaster after another. Perhaps the worst crisis came after he had 'bought up' the Oakland Oaks basketball team. In September 1968 he was suddenly confronted with an overdraft of a quarter of a million pounds for which he had to find the money within 24 hours. He managed it, but a year later the Oakland Oaks franchise hit total collapse and he was faced with either bankruptcy or a heavy bill.

After he had put things right spiritually the franchise was bought, thus saving him from the disgrace of bankruptcy.

His marriage had also reached a crisis point. It had completely disintegrated through a whole series of disillusionments, disappointments and falling out of love. 'Shirley and I just didn't love each other. We lived together in the same house but there was little between us except anxieties, animosities and mutual blame. I blamed Shirley for my downfall and, of course, she felt I had totally let her down as a spritual leader and husband and that I had become somebody else totally – and in many ways I had. She was more aware than any other human being of my hypocrisy. There were times when there was almost no affection between us and I got tired of being blamed for it all. I felt that she was just as much to blame as I and so we would have loud arguments, although I never hit her except, I think once. Then my children were also aware that their father was leading a two or three faced life. They saw one Pat Boone at home, another Pat Boone at church and another Pat Boone on television – and wondered how many Pat Boones there were! I had lost a lot of their respect and it was just a matter of time till the whole family disintegrated.'

'I realized that only a miracle could put our family and marriage back together and also give my career any meaning. I began to cry out for a miracle but the trouble was my whole teaching in the Church of Christ was that miracles don't happen, that God went out of the miracle business towards the close of the first century as His Word was written. Any miracles that did happen were to confirm that it was His Word, and after that we were left on our own to read, understand and practice the Bible. He wouldn't intervene in people's lives in any supernatural or miraculous way. And yet I knew if God didn't intervene, it was all over for me.'

'One by one the pieces began to fall into place and I started talking to God. One day when I spoke to God – I began to cry! I heard the sound of my own voice talking to God really earnestly and with a sense that he was hearing me! I didn't expect to cry, something just broke within me. I began to ask God to move into my life, save my marriage, bring my family back together, give my career some purpose and also – hopefully – solve these financial problems.'

'After that I began to get involved in Bible study groups and prayer groups in homes and saw that our little Church of Christ didn't have the franchise on Christianity. More and more I realized that I had lived in a very narrow little doctrinaire World and that there was a whole dimension and realm of relationship with God which I had been closed to because of my own lack of understanding. So, a time came when I just asked the Lord to take over. I said, "I give up trying to place limits on it; you do it." I realized this might mean me giving up my career and material things. But I had reached the stage where I had little left that was of value to me. I just asked God to take me and He baptized me in the Holy Spirit, which was as simple and real an operation as when He saved me . . . That was in 1969.'

About four years later Pat Boone returned to England with the role of pop superstar behind him and as a Christian 'entertainer' as his new objective in life.

It was a whirlwind tour of the UK that attracted

capacity houses for 'Come Together' in seven different centres and a seemingly endless onslaught of interviews. He had a minimum of sleep but that hardly sapped any of his enthusiasm for the mission.

'Christianity does play an important role in my life but that's not to say that I'm not still entertaining,' he said. However, today Pat Boone's act has a new emphasis as he explains; 'A recent national political survey showed that America's mothers are more concerned about the urgent problems of keeping the family together, than about drugs, pornography, violence or educational snarls. How can it be done today? We've asked the same question; we're all looking for an answer. We live in Hollywood California. We have four daughters. All around us we see kids just like ours 'turning on', dropping out, running away and messing up. Close friends are seeing their marriages dissolve and their families disintegrate.

We had to find the answers. And we have! They work; they're simple; they're exciting and they're fun! We share these fundamental answers with our listeners. We do it the only way we know – from the Boone Family – with love and music!'

'Christ's return for His own will be the most profound moment in all history and it is, I believe, very near . . . all creation is now breathlessly awaiting that glorious rapture! This thrilling message must be proclaimed urgently by song and by word right now to Christians as well as to those friends who are not regular church-goers.'

II: Anita Bryant - 'Miss Oklahoma'

'If you don't bring my daughter and that baby round, I'll kill you!' said the irate baby's Grandpa as he shook his fist and swore at the Doctor. But the impulsive remarks were ignored by the Doctor as he continued earnestly to endeavour to save the young mother's life who had just given birth to a nine pound baby – black and swollen with poison – apparently dead.

Shifting attention from the mother to this sad baby, the Doctor demanded iced water, strong coffee and whisky from the two worried grandparents. The baby's head was dipped into the iced water catching the breath of the sad, new born form. The Doctor simultaneously slapped the baby's bottom stimulating a weak cry. 'Now get that coffee and whisky down that baby's mouth somehow!' he told the anxious grandparents, 'While I take care of your daughter.'

Although apparently hopeless, grandpa and grandma patiently and persistently kept pouring tiny amounts of liquid down the baby's mouth. Suddenly it all erupted – coffee, whisky and the poison too! Glancing around, the Doctor said, 'She might live!' ... And indeed she did! Such was the dramatic entrance into the World of Anita Bryant.

She was born into the raw, rugged Oklahoma oil country, the daughter of Warren and Leonora Bryant. Anita's father was a tall, tough exuberant oil field roust-

about from Oklahoma City. When Anita was born her mother was only 18 and her father 19. Eighteen months later Anita's sister Sandy Jean joined the family. As the time of Anita's birth had drawn near her pregnant mother felt very homesick. So, on her visit to her parent's house in Barnsdall, baby Anita was dramatically born.

Her grandfather encouraged the young Anita in her early years to sing. With her cousins and sister Sandy she spent hours learning songs from the radio. The high spot of the week was listening to the 'Grand Ole Opry' programme originating from Nashville, Tennessee every Saturday night. The kids loved to sing the old Opry numbers especially the ones by Little Jimmie Dickens. Using the back porch for a stage, Anita would delight her young cousins with such classics as 'Sleeping at the foot of the bed,' and 'Take an old cold tater and wait!'

Her first public appearance was at the tender age of two years! Uninhibited – too young to be shy – she startled the congregation of Barnsdall Baptist Church with her charming version of 'Jesus loves me!' And she had an unusually big voice for a two year old!

Sadly, soon after her sister was born, their parents divorced. The pressures of family life were just too much for the young marriage to endure. Her father joined the army while her mother took the girls to live with their grandparents. Tragedy soon followed again. Anita's grandfather, who had always earned a good living with one of the major oil refineries, was caught in a major explosion which killed several men. He escaped with his life, but the hot tar that had sluiced across his face destroyed his eyesight. Her big, brash, family-loving Grandfather – the tough oilman who could 'out-cuss' anybody else on the job – was still fairly young when overnight he found himself totally helpless and dependant. Soon after this tragedy, however, he experienced a Christian Conversion . . . his tragedy was turned to triumph! 'I had to get my eyes put out before I could really see!' he told his grandchildren. Actually it was his wife's faith that guided him to God. When his need was greatest – it had never wavered. Her grandparents' Christ-centered faith deeply impressed the young Anita.

Anita's parents re-married when she was three, which delighted her and her sister. In addition, opportunities in singing, even at such a young age were increasing with each year. She also developed another interest. At weekends she learned to ride horses. Her favourite was a palomino named Old Pet. She never dreamed, as she taught herself to ride bareback, that she was helping herself train for the rodeo work she would do later.

At the 1949 high school senior class party, dressed in a 'grass' skirt her mother made, Anita sang, 'I wanna go back to my little grass shack in Kealakekua, Hawaii'. This was followed by her appearance at the school's PTA meeting singing, 'Feudin' Fussin', and Fightin' '. As the bookings increased, so too, Anita's aspirations grew. 'I'm going to be a star' she said.

Dressed in a cowboy costume she entered a radio talent show in Duncan, Oklahoma. The contest lasted 6 or 8 weeks and each week the eight-year-old Anita walked off with an exciting prize for her rendition of 'Bonaparte's retreat' or a similar classic country song. With each success she gained confidence . . . radio . . . TV . . . stage . . . opportunities galore! She started a regular spot on a country music show on TV entitled 'Sooner Shindig' and then another called 'The Scotty Hurrell Show' followed. When Scotty moved on, Anita was given the slot. Every Friday night she had her own 15 minute programme . . . And she was only 12 years old!

Life was now turning for the good, Anita felt, after such a rough start.

At the age 12 the independent, up-and-coming singing star committed her life to Jesus Christ. 'Every thing in my life seemed to be on the right track just as I'd have it be. Then the blow fell. Sandy and and I learned that our parents intended to divorce one another for the second time! 'We felt stunned and as desolate as Mother, and probably Daddy, must have felt.' Anita recalls, 'For the first time in my life I came to God in real anguish . . . then the peace of God that passes all understanding came at last . . .'

In 1953 she cut her first record – a single called 'Somebody cares'. This simple little sacred song encouraged the young teenager Anita to approach the major record companies and also the Hollywood movie companies . . . without success. In the meantime her mother re-married and the family moved to Tulsa where Anita began regular appearances on the 'Chris Lane TV Show'. It was soon followed by regular appearances on the important 'Arthur Godfrey CBS TV Show' originating from New York. During her last year at High School she signed with the MCA agency and secured a recording contract with Carlton Records.

Soon another phase in her career blossomed – she entered the 'Miss Tulsa Beauty Contest' and won! . . . next came 'The Miss Oklahoma' prize which she won too . . . then in the exciting 'Miss America' contest she finished runner-up for the winner's crown.

The following year the record she had cut for Carlton Records 'Till there was you' moved up to the million mark in sales. Important TV and personal appearances (such as the Dick Clark Bandstand) followed to back up her first hit. In Miami she appeared in a great convention which included Connie Francis, Pat Boone, Errol

Garner, Peggy Lee, Frank Sinatra and the Kirby Stone Four – to name a few! It was in Miami she met and fell in love with an important disc jockey Bob Green. They subsequently married amid much publicity.

During those years of Hit Parade popularity, Anita moved away from her early years' country music heritage, and joined 'chart toppers' such as Pat Boone, Bobby Rydell, Bobby Darin, and Paul Anka on various major spectaculars. Other single hits followed such as 'In my little corner of the World" and 'Paper Roses' which gave Anita international star status. In those few years she sold over three million single records.

Network TV appearances followed with Jimmy Dean, Tennessee Ernie Ford, Ed Sullivan and many others. Within a year Anita was voted 'Best vocalist of the Year' by the Academy of Television Arts and Sciences.

For seven consecutive years she was the singing attraction on comedian Bob Hope's regular holiday tours to remote US armed forces bases such as Korea and Vietnam. Anita's Christian love and compassion were demonstrated over and over again as she visited the hospitals of the wounded. On these tours she would renew acquaintances with Billy Graham, George Beverly Shea, and Cliff Barrows – her good friends. Highlights of these tours were the exciting command performances before the King and Queen of Thailand.

The stage has found Anita essaying such roles as 'Annie' in 'Annie Get Your Gun' and Maria' in 'The Sound of Music,' and many others.

As a native of Oklahoma, Anita became the youngest women ever to be named to the Oklahoma Hall of Fame. She is also the youngest American ever to receive the USO Silver Medallion Award. For her patriotic endeavours she received the 1969 Freedom Leadership Award from Freedoms Foundation at Valley Forge.

After she was signed up by major record company Columbia Records, Anita again returned to her musical 'homeground'. Her rich, warm voice was more at home in simple country ballads than in the popular songs she took to the top of the hit parade charts. Country ballads were a natural, spontaneous expression of the traditions deeply rooted in her rural Oklahoma upbringing. However, she is even more at home singing songs about her personal faith in Jesus Christ. 'This music,' explains Anita, 'is more than entertainment. It is part of me. Ever since I first sang in the choir of my grandparents church in Tishomingo, Oklahoma, I've always wanted to record sacred songs. I've sung many of these songs in churches and at revivals. They are a testament of my faith.' Her association with Word Records has helped her share these songs of testimony with millions of people via her beautiful albums. In elaboration of her comment that these songs of testimony are more than 'mere entertainment', she recalls a tense but gratifying experience in the early sixties at Fort Lauderdale, Florida. It was there that students from all over the country gathered to celebrate the end of the school year. Anita remembers, 'They go for a good time, but some of them let their spirits get a little out of hand. Local citizens were upset by the noisy disturbances some of the boys were making in the streets. Fortunately, the famous religious leader, Billy Graham was in the area, so Fort Lauderdale authorities asked him to speak a few words of moderation to the boys. Mr. Graham knew I was at home in Miami just a few miles away, and he asked me to sing some religious songs after his talk. Frankly, I was a little frightened at first – boys were standing around near the beach with beer cans in their hands. When they were in a calmer mood, I sang two of my favourites, "It took a miracle" and "If you know the Lord", and the

27

youngsters were really moved! They listened respectfully to those songs, and moved away quietly after our impromptu revival.'

The story of Anita Bryant is a thrilling challenge and inspiration. It's a long way from rural Oklahoma to the White House but she made it in only 28 years when she lifted her world-famous voice in a fervent rendition of the 'Battle Hymn of the Republic' before the President, who then led the assembly in a standing ovation. Anita has appeared many, many times at the White House, has joined evangelists Billy Graham and Oral Roberts in their evangelistic crusades, and for many years toured with Bob Hope in his overseas Christmas Shows. Yes, the small time country girl has evolved into a hardworking, successful performer, a devoted wife and mother, but first and foremost, an active, witnessing Christian.

III: Johnny Cash - 'The Tall Dark Troubador'

The term 'living legend' has often been used in the Music Industry, and often the subject does not deserve the label . . . But that could not be said of Johnny Cash.

In every tour of the United Kingdom, ticket applications always pour in to organizers for concert seats to see the legendary Johnny Cash. No other entertainer in the world today can evoke such tremendous loyalty from his fans. Some would gladly travel several hundred miles to be present at a performance by this dynamic singer. Rich and poor, professional people and artisans, old and young flock to see and hear this man.

The secret of Johnny Cash's appeal is not hard to identify. It lies in his tremendous integrity. This one transcending quality shines through, both on and off the stage, in his role as an entertainer and as a human being. His long climb from obscurity in Memphis to the heights of international stardom has been far from easy. Cash is one artist who has paid his dues in real blood, sweat, and tears.

He was born on the 26th February, 1932, in the little hamlet of Kingsland, Arkansas, the son of a share-cropping family who *knew* hard times. In fact, the sturdy Arkansas family of Ray and Carrie Cash knew nothing but hard times when Johnny was in his infancy. This was the time of the great American Depres-

sion and the family, which at its peak numbered seven, literally starved more than once. One time, at least, this nearly came to its logical conclusion but always somehow Carrie and Ray managed to provide enough food for their children but often it was a close thing. In this atmosphere of a continual struggle for survival, the likes of which is almost impossible to comprehend today, it is no small wonder that Johnny Cash has a serious outlook on life.

In the winter of 1935, Ray Cash placed his wife, and six children and a few belongings in an old pick-up truck and headed on up the road. President Franklin D. Roosevelt, as part of the 'New Deal' programme, had opened up Dyess Colony – 14,000 acres of scrubland in the north-eastern corner of the state. Anyone prepared to clear the land would get 20 acres, a house, a barn and a mule! As a teenager Johnny picked cotton, 350 pounds a day, dragging a 9 foot sack down the tangled rows. He later hauled two 5-gallon water jugs for the levee work gangs on the banks of the Tyronza River. 'They kept me running as fast as I could but I'd turn on the radios in the workman's cars when I was getting the water, and slip in and listen to the country songs!'

In July 1950, at the age of 18 Johnny enlisted in the US Air Force. This was quite a logical move for a poor, Southern, farm boy. The work was steady (which was the biggest appeal in a still depressed South) and the pay was good. For the first time Johnny saw the outside world as it really was, and only then did he realize that there was more to life than just the fight against starvation. Trained as a radio-intercept operator, he was sent to Germany where he bought his first guitar. After four years he was demobilized with the rank of staff sergeant and the ability (which he still retains to this day) to read Morse code at the rate of sixty words a minute.

When in 1954 he left the service, like so many farm boys, he went to the city. In this case it was Memphis. However, unlike many contemporaries he was not satisfied with the first available job he could get. Besides selling electrical appliances, he also took a radio announcer's course as he felt some facet of show business was to be his destiny, and this was a good solid foundation on which to build his career. Johnny had begun singing to his colleagues in the Air Force, and at the back of his mind he had the notion of being a singing star though he realized this was aiming high.

He also searched for a chance to sing, trying three times for an audition with 'Sun Records'. Through Sun's doors had walked Elvis Presley, Jerry Lee Lewis, Roy Orbison, Conway Twitty, Carl Perkins . . . and now it was Johnny Cash's turn. After a year of waiting his first release 'Cry, Cry, Cry' sold 100,000 copies – mostly in the South and particularly in Texas – and Cash was on his way! A few months later, in early 1956, Sun released a third Cash single 'I walk the line', a million seller, it shot Johnny into prominence. This, in turn, was followed by 'Ballad of a Teenage Queen' which finally established his name in the international market. In August 1958, having provided 'Sun Records' with a string of successful hit records during his three year contract, Johnny signed with 'Columbia Records'. Demand for his records increased. Not one of his 'Columbia' albums sold less than 100,000 each! In 1970 alone he sold 6,000,000 records in that single year.

A complex spirit who found the entire world a little claustrophobic, Johnny was stretched even more taughtly by the demands placed on him by his success. The pressures of touring, twice nightly performances, recording, radio, and television all combined to squeeze in upon him. In 1961 he turned to a stimulant to keep up. To relax he then needed a tranquillizer. Soon he was locked into the cruel circle of drugs. One night in 1967 stopped him cold. 'I woke up in jail in Georgia and didn't remember how I got there!' A policeman had found him wandering the streets and brought him in to sleep it off.

On stage he would prance around like a big, nervous cat, fondling his guitar one minute then throwing it around his neck a second later, and he wasn't too worried about spicing his introductions with the odd obscenity.

He earned a bad reputation for being unreliable because of his long addiction to pep pills. Off stage he was, on occasions, a warm human being with a big heart. Other times he would be just plain mean! Beneath his scarred exterior (the scar on his chin is the result of a skin complaint – not a knife wound) which was hewn out of hardship, pep pills, hunger, and frustrations lay a gentle spirit seeking fulfilment. *Life* magazine described Cash and his music in the following lines, 'His face looks ruined, his lean body whipped out. He sings off-key, of bygone days that many of his listeners can't even remember: railroads, hobos, the open road.'

A decline in popularity set in following a series of mediocre recordings. Something was obviously wrong. His friendship and musical associations with folk-balladeer Bob Dylan began to receive publicity and Johnny slowly became accepted by the Greenwich Village folkies. They liked his involvement with various social causes, especially with the plight of the American Indian. Indeed, he has a streak of Cherokee blood running through his veins. In addition to his Indian activities, Johnny became very much involved with the American Penal System. He donated 5,000 dollars for a chapel to be built at the infamous Cummins Prison Farm in Arkansas. The *New York Times* said of Cash, 'He's the first angry man of country songsters, the first grim and gutsy pusher of social causes.' *Time* magazine summed the attitude of his songs up . . . 'Life both in and out of prisons is a kind of sentence to be served.'

In reply to such statements, Cash replies, 'People like my songs because there's *realism* in them, unlike most songs. They have true human emotions as well as being stories . . . My music is more of a personal thing than a vehicle to use to carry messages. It's mainly something to be enjoyed. Life can be a sentence but you can enjoy it if you *want* to, and I've enjoyed most of it.' Thus, Johnny has ridden many causes. When he can, he puts on benefit performances at the reservations to raise money for the neglected Indian. His compassion for convicts often haunts his songs, and he has played many of the big penitentiaries including San Quentin and Folsom Prison. 'I don't see anything good come out of a prison,' he argues, 'You put them in like animals and tear the soul and guts out of them, and let them out worse than when they went in!' This compassion for his fellow man has struck a responsive chord in the hearts of all those who hear his music. His forthright honesty has enabled him not only to bridge the gap between generations, but to break down some barriers that divide contemporary society.

About the time of Johnny's personal failure he had a spiritual experience that changed the direction of his life. A New Life style developed. Indeed, new life obviously came to his haggard frame.

After his first marriage collapsed, he married June Carter in 1968. She herself was an impressive talent in Country Music. She was the youngest daughter of Mother Maybelle Carter of the legendary Carter Family of the 1920's and 30's. June sang and picked guitar on Nashville's renowned radio programme the 'Grand Ole Opry' for 17 years and had been with John in the Cash show.

In 1970 Johnny Cash Junior was born to this couple who were determined, by God's grace to walk in their Savour's footsteps. 'Photoplay' magazine reported: 'About a week before the baby was born, Billy Graham was down here, and I visited with him,' Johnny pensively remarked, 'He's been a good friend of mine and has prayed for me a lot. Anyway, I told him how much I wanted this baby and how I hoped it would be a boy. And Billy Graham, being the good friend that he is, said, "John I hope God hears your prayers. I know He'll listen to you cause you've got an honest heart!" He also told me he'd pray specially for June and me these next weeks. Well, I appreciate the prayers and I want all my friends to know that I am most grateful to them for taking time to talk to my Jesus about my family ... I also told Dr. Graham that the greatest humiliation I've ever suffered was *worth* it if my example can keep just one person from touching drugs. Now I'm going to build a Chapel to the Lord in my home town of Hendersonville (just outside of Nashville) to show Him how much I appreciate the way He has seen fit to bless me,' Johnny said, visibly touched ... 'The name of the Lord is as commonplace in the Cash home as black-eyed peas on their dinner table.' Since those days John and June have spiritually progressed even further in the Faith according to all reports.

The year previous to the birth of his son, Johnny was earning a reported 3,000,000 dollars from record royalties and concert appearances and since then his popularity has increased. He has walked away with almost every award the music industry has given. Johnny Cash is a folk-hero today – a legend in his own lifetime.

On the completion of his European tour in the autumn of 1972 Johnny and June flew to Boiling Springs, North Carolina, where the Gardner-Webb College conferred on him the honorary degree of Doctor of Humanities in recognition of humanitarian services and reforms. An honour previously bestowed on his friend, Billy Graham.

In the winter of 1972 Johnny and June travelled to

Israel to undertake location filming for a documentary depicting the life of his Lord and Saviour-Jesus Christ. The film carries a dramatic soundtrack narration by Johnny reading from the Gospels.

This is the man who's made millions from songs of blood, sweat, tears, trains, Indians, booze ... life! But today's Cash is different! He believes in Christ and he's out to promote Jesus and to discover what *He* really meant when He uttered His immortal words nearly 2,000 years ago. Cash is a folk-singer of the highest order. When he wraps his tortured voice round the lyrics of any song you know that every last syllable is steeped in sincerity. 'I don't hold any political views,' he states emphatically, 'I sing songs and do the job I'm cut out to do. I just wish people could learn to live in peace with each other. I often sit and think how much blood has been shed because of the misinterpretation of Christ's words ... I've seen the Light! ... I've always been a deeply religious person but these days the light's shining a little brighter!'

Shirley Boone (Pat's wife) writes, 'Johnny Cash ... has just recently been filled with the Holy Spirit, as has his wife June, and soon after, as he completed a concert in Holland, he felt so strongly moved by the Lord that he gave an 'altar call'. In other words, at the end of his performance Johnny, surprising himself perhaps as much as his audience, but sensing their spiritual hunger, extended God's great invitation. Like a tent-meeting evangelist, he urged his listeners to come forward and accept salvation through Christ. And in that foreign city, from among those who'd come to find entertainment rather than Jesus, an estimated 2,000 people responded! Johnny was stunned. He'd never given an altar call before and he certainly hadn't intended to give one as his concert 'encore'. Yet, because he'd previously asked the Lord to take charge of his life, the Lord has used him gloriously.'

This was just the beginning of a new, fulfilling and unending adventure for the tall, dark, amiable troubadour from the dirt farm of Kingsland.

IV: Jimmie Davis - 'The Singing Governor of Louisana'

Where does a legend begin? The Jimmie Houstan Davis legend began on 9th November 1902 in a small, humble 'Shotgun' cabin nestled in the rural, red clay hills of Beech Springs, Quitman, Northern Louisiana. If one was to return there today one would realize that a person's beginnings have much to say about the man. Today the cabin is a monument, but once it was a bare roof and three rooms that housed a sharecropper, his wife, eleven children, and assorted relatives! The land was wild; it is today. There are no electric lines. Very few people live in these parts. The pines, all around, grow tall and gaze down in evergreen silence. Civilization and the 20th Century seem a million miles away. What do people who occupy this land have? They have each other . . . They have the land . . . And they have a deep rooted faith in the Lord their God . . . They believe He watches and cares for His own even during times of adversity and trouble. It's then, as they lean on Him, they prove Him to be 'a very present help in time of trouble.' . . . And that's what Jimmie Davis is all about. A man who has learned to quietly lean and commune with his Maker and Saviour.

Much of the Jimmie Davis career mirrors the traditional American dream. The 'rags to riches' theme: the poor farm boy who became the Governor of the mighty State of Louisiana. He grew up close to the soil working

his hoe in the fields or wandering in the woods. Early in life, as he proved the Lord, he developed a deep faith, and also in his free moments developed a love of singing.

To fulfil his destiny, as both a singer of great fame and a public official commanding great respect and loyalty, Jimmie began his travels from the farm where his sharecropping parents raised their eleven children. *Time* magazine once breezily described Jimmie as one who has 'always had the knack of strumming his way toward the top'; but such a description makes his journey sound far easier than it has actually been. The truth is that his earlier years challenged his perseverance and courage at every bend of the road.

At Louisiana College in Pineville he had only one shirt which he washed every night, ironed every morning, and wore every day. Even when the struggling, earnest Davis won his Bachelor's Degree, he yearned for still more learning, hoping he might someday serve his fellow man to the very limits of his God-given potential. However, his continuing education was necessarily interrupted by several terms as a history teacher and athletic coach while he scraped together enough money to go to the Louisiana State University. Despite the need to save he would always send home more than a little of his wages to aid the education of his younger brothers and sisters.

He was never happier than when he was singing and writing songs. He started appearing on several local radio stations and then the giant Decca Record Company heard him and signed him to a contract in the mid 30's after a short spell with RCA Victor. His fidelity and popularity is clear from the fact that he stayed with the same record company for nearly 40 years.

During the late 30's and early 40's he was lured to the bright lights of Hollywood and made appearances in several movies but the 'big-time' doors were closed to him. Another vocation was to be his destiny.

Returning to Louisiana he made a big name for himself in country music. Then he was bitten by the political bug. He ran for Police Commissioner of Shreveport, La., and in 1938 was elected. He served four years and was next elected in 1942 to a six-year term on the Louisiana Public Service Commission. He served for two years then resigned to run for Governor. He was elected and served until 1948. He was re-elected in 1960 and served until 1964. In Louisiana, a governor cannot succeed himself.

Over the years Jimmie kept recording and performing, except while he was the Governor because he felt a great obligation to those who elected him. In the early years he 'plugged along' until in 1939 he caught the imagination of the depression-ridden world with a simple song he wrote entitled 'You are my Sunshine'. This great sing-along standard has been recorded hundreds of times and has sold in the millions. It must rate as one of the World's most popular melodies ever! It was reported that, even 30 years after he wrote it, the song was earning £5,000 per year in royalties. It has been so continuously popular that he has had to record it three different times for Decca himself.

About twenty years ago Jimmie felt an inner calling to write and sing Gospel Music. As a result he switched from country to gospel music. During that time he has written many songs which are becoming evergreen gospel favourites such as 'Someone to Care', 'Sheltered in His Arms', 'Sweet Mystery', 'Wait for an Answer', 'By His Stripes we are Healed', 'He's the Saviour of the World', etc. 'I feel in Gospel Singing I can render a ministry, and that is why I prefer it to anything I have ever done in my life,' Jimmie once commented.

Jimmie has sung Gospel Music throughout the USA for more than 20 years. Even while Governor he was never completely free of singing and preaching engagements in churches. He said, 'I never overlook an opportunity to preach the gospel and share the message of a sacred song.'

In 1964, in his last year in the Governor's mansion his many friends gave him a testimonial dinner and pledged to build a church to be named after him. So the 'Jimmie Davis Tabernacle', one of the most beautiful non-denominational churches in the World, was completed and dedicated to the service of the Lord on 16th May 1965. It is situated on the site of his old home place (where he grew up) on Peckerwood Hill between Quitman and Jonesboro, Louisiana. Jimmie frequently sings and preaches the gospel at the beautiful church.

In 1967 his dear wife Alvern Adams died after they had shared many years of happy marriage. They had lived with their son in Baton Rouge where Jimmie was kept busy with his public relations business as well as his public duties. He also raises cattle and horses on his farm which is managed by his son Jimmie Jnr. In addition, he is kept busy with the music publishing companies he owns.

In 1972 he joined the literally very select handful of people to be elected to the Country Music Hall of Fame. A great and rare privilege, especially for a living person. Living legends are rare but Jimmie Davis is indeed a legend in his own time. At the age of 73 years he was still very active, singing, recording, and indeed even ran unsuccessfully for the office of Governor of Louisiana for the 3rd time! Assisting in his political career was his new bride Anna Gordon (one of the original members of the Christian singing group 'The Chuck Wagon Gang' which was founded in 1936). Jimmie still confirms that his first love is to sing the Gospel and proved that by even singing Gospel Music at his political rallies.

He became a top country music artist, two-time Governor of Louisiana, and composer of many hits but now he is in his 20th year of composing and performing Gospel Music. Jimmie concludes, 'Singing Gospel Music has given me greater pleasure than anything I have ever done. I enjoyed my two terms as Governor. It was a great challenge. But I've enjoyed singing the Gospel best! '

Down through the years the songs of Jimmie Davis have touched many lives and in more than a few instances proved to be a help to troubled men and women. His strength of character has never manifested itself in the form of a stern manner. Indeed, his inward faith and calm is reflected in gentleness and thoughtful consideration of others. The sincerity of his own convictions is the secret of his evangelistic persuasiveness in leading his listeners to the paths of righteousness.

To the son of a humble Louisiana sharecropper (with 11 children) who rose to the head of his State, God has given the gift of magnificent self-expression and Jimmie's use of that gift, even in the eventide of his busy life, must surely give His Saviour reason to be greatly pleased.

V: Skeeter Davis - 'The Sunshine Gal'

The World of Country Music is certainly grateful for the talent of Skeeter Davis. For twenty years now she has brought untold hours of sunshine and musical pleasure to millions of fans. Sweet and unassuming, this girl from Dry Ridge, Kentucky, has become one of the most sought after celebrities of Nashville, Tennessee. She is in constant demand for personal appearances both in the USA and abroad.

What is it that makes a person warm and friendly? All who have met Skeeter testify to the fact that gallons of warmth and friendliness ooze from her charming personality. Warmth and friendliness are an integral part of her behaviour and conversation – indeed, her whole person! Christ once said that what shows in a person's life is exactly what is in that person's heart. No one would deny that Skeeter Davis has a warm and friendly heart. Such qualities come from her real, dynamic, heart-felt faith in God and Christ as her Saviour.

Articles about Skeeter in 'Country Music People' magazine by the editor Bob Powel, and colleague Tony Byworth, have constantly stressed this winsome character of hers. Indeed Bob described Skeeter 'without fear of contradiction . . . one of the best loved people of Nashville. If you don't know why, then quite simply you haven't met her. She is one of the sweetest, unaffected people there is. In fact she is so nice that it is almost

impossible to believe that she has been in the back-biting music business for over twenty years, not only in it, but very near the top.' That is praise indeed!

One of Skeeter's Nashville colleagues Dolly Parton describes her like this, 'I think I'll call her sunshine. She's as warm and friendly as a summer day, and the sunshine of her smile and glowing personality add warmth and beauty to the world she lives in and to those she includes in it. I have always been a fan of Skeeter's, more as a person than an artist, even though I think she is a great performer. She sings great and adds so much to our business, but you have to know her as a person to really appreciate her greatness and beauty.'

A vivacious blonde Kentuckian, Skeeter Davis (she was actually christened Mary Frances, but can't remember back to the day when she didn't have the nickname Skeeter) has had her best selling records with sad songs. Those who know her well shake their heads and grin at the fact that Skeeter has scored her greatest successes with tearful tunes like 'The End of the World', 'I Forgot more than you'll ever know', and 'My Last Date (with you)', when as a matter of fact, Skeeter's just about the most cheerful, talkative, bubbling gal around!

Where did such winsomeness come from? This chapter may explain. It is the true story of what faith in God can produce in the life of a person. The Bible says, 'Christ in you – The Hope of Glory!' Skeeter literally wears her heart on her sleeve. On her clothes and baggage can be seen dozens of stickers declaring, 'I am a Jesus Person,', or 'Jesus loves you', etc. Someone once asked her if she was 'into Jesus'. 'No', came the reply, 'Jesus is into me' . . . 'If you are saved,' she explains, 'and Jesus is in your life then there is a definite spiritual change in your life. You are a Child of God when you accept Jesus as your Saviour. The Apostle John said: "to as many as receive Him (Jesus) to them He gives the right to be called the Children of God". It's certainly different once you've accepted Christ . . . The theme of Christianity is "God is Love" – and I have it on a little necklace I wear everywhere!'

Skeeter was born on a farm in Dry Ridge, Kentucky, on the 30th December, 1931, the first of seven children. 'My daddy always said we were about average people back in Kentucky, but I think really we were probably below average. When you're poor like that, it leaves you with a little more heart.'

She started singing in early childhood with no formal voice training. She recalls with a smile, 'My first public performance (outside of the one room schoolroom when I was in the first grade) was at the Cincinnati Zoo when I was five years old. The eighth grade graduating class went on a class trip from Dry Ridge, Kentucky – at least fifty or sixty miles (before the interstate). Since I was the only one in the first grade, they took me along as their mascot – since they didn't have a dog! They all encouraged me to sing and I'd sing my favourite song at the time 'Pop goes the weasel'. It wasn't a number one record on any chart but I sure got a big hand and I'd sing my little heart out! The class would stand me out in front of everybody and have me sing and people would give me nickles and dimes and applause. The kids took the money – I got to keep the applause. I knew from the beginning it was the applause that thrilled me! That was like being hugged by a lot of people or I guess it was kind of like being loved. I had not experienced anything like that before, and I was loving everybody back with my song – silly little song that it was. Now I sing a different song.'

Skeeter Davis moved into a world rather distant from that little town – so tiny, in fact, that most road maps ignore it. 'I didn't have a religious upbringing,' Skeeter explained, 'in fact to be honest my father was an alcoholic who has since been converted, which I think is just an answer to prayer . . . it took a long time. But I went to Sunday School and I was always conscious that God had His hand on my life and had a purpose for it although I did not know Him.'

Skeeter's friend and pastor, Rev. Robert Daugherty

continues, 'During a revival service in a little country church in Kentucky as a teenage girl she felt the presence of God speak to her heart through some of the great hymns and sacred songs. At the close of the Bible message delivered by the evangelist she accepted the preacher's invitation to put her faith and trust in God and her hand in the nail scarred hand of Jesus Christ. Since that night she has walked hand in hand with Jesus through many joyous and many tragic experiences. Her deep convictions and profound faith in God have been sorely tested, but her faith has stood the test; it has never wavered and never failed. On the contrary her faith only grows stronger with each trial and tribulation. It seems life has heaped more burdens and disappointments upon her than one person could bear and yet she comes through it all with her hand still in the hand of Jesus.'

She started singing in high school with her partner, Billy Jack Davis, and in 1956 had their first smash hit with 'I forgot more than you'll ever know'. Unfortunately a short time later Billy Jack died in a car accident and Skeeter's interest in her career came to an abrupt halt. Her pastor remembers, 'Billy Jack and Skeeter were a team until Billy Jack was killed in an auto accident; they seemed just like two girls with one soul. Billy Jack felt the presence and call of God at the same time and in the same manner as Skeeter. She had the same kind of faith and convictions as Skeeter, she, too, walked hand in hand with Jesus.'

In time Skeeter re-adjusted to life and to her music and the sun shone through again. Skeeter continued as a single act and auditioned for and gained her own radio show on WLAX in Lexington, Kentucky. She then soon moved over to WJR in Detroit where she was heard by a much wider audience. She gained further experience with regular stints on WCOP-TV and WKAC-TV in Cincinnati, and then on WWVA, Wheeling, West Virginia's renowned broadcast outlet.

After her return to show business she toured very successfully with Ernest Tubb and his Texas Troubadours and in 1959 she was named 'Most Promising Female Country Vocalist' and was made a permanent member of the 'Grand Ole Opry.'

Skeeter has been with RCA Victor records since her beginning, and she has given them one hit after another. Her biggest hit to date is her million seller 'The End of The World'. It was a giant success, not only in the UK but all over the World. You might say the 'End' was really the 'Beginning'. Other successful recordings have been, 'Set Him Free', 'Last Date', 'I can't Stay Mad at You', 'What Does it Take', 'I'm a Lover Not a Fighter', 'Bridge Over Troubled Waters', 'Bus Fare to Kentucky', and 'Love Takes a Lot of My Time'. She has also recorded about thirty albums.

Her numerous hits, led to appearances on many of the USA's top television shows, including the Dick Clark Show, the Jimmy Dean Show and two evangelistic TV specials for Oral Roberts as well as in films like 'Forty Acre Feud'.

She is at home on any stage she appears on – from the Grand Ole Opry to Wembley Pool, from Carnegie Hall to the Royal Albert Hall. She has a tremendous appeal to people of all ages and types. She not only sings, but she entertains and spreads her message of love that springs from a deep, sincere devotion to God that wins people with her personality and warmth.

Skeeter has many awards to her credit, including a Grammy Award and many other Grammy nominations. She has also won BMI Awards for songwriting, and been given the Peter DeRose Award for her moving

'Somebody Loves You' .... and as the years pass her popularity increases.

When asked about her future Skeeter quoted the promise of Romans 8:28, 'For we know that all things work together for good to those that love God and who are called according to His purposes.'

From WSM Radio, home of the 'Grand Ole Opry', Ott Divine stated, 'Sincerity is the word for Skeeter Davis. This is the one attribute more responsible for her success in country music than any other. It has gained for her a warm spot in the hearts of millions. Today, Skeeter Davis is a shining example of the singers of tomorrow. If sincerity, devotion to family, love of people and warmth of heart are the requirements of a country music star, then Skeeter rates Number One in her field.'

However, I won't finish there, I'll let Rev. Robert Daugherty conclude her story; 'As her pastor, I rejoice that her faith and convictions are reflected both in her private life and her professional life. Her faith and beliefs control her life in every way. She does not alter her beliefs to coincide with her professional career; but alters her professional career to coincide with her beliefs. For all the years I have known her, Skeeter Davis has remained true to her convictions. She has kept the faith. Where and how does the story end? No one will know the number of hearts that will be touched or the lives that have been blessed ... As far as Skeeter is concerned she will continue to walk hand in hand with Jesus throughout this life and the life to come. You might conclude by saying, 'And she lived happily everlastingly!'

VI: Tennessee Ernie Ford - 'The Tennessee Peapicker'

'Gospel hymns bring us an age old message in beautiful music. It's good music because the message from the Gospel is always one that lies true to my heart' . . . so says the evergreen Ernie Ford.

Of all the fine things that are said about Tennessee Ernie Ford, perhaps the closest to his heart is this: among the many millions of people who regard religious music as a cherished part of their spiritual life, he is universally recognized as one of the foremost reverential singers. Thanks to the many recordings he has made, countless thousands every day listen to Ernie's rich baritone recitals of their favourite hymns, spirituals and gospel songs. Always Tennessee Ernie Ford displays the taste, reverence and enthusiasm which evokes the warmest possible response from his many, many listeners.

Tennessee Ernie declares, 'I have never made any secret about enjoying religion. And I've sure never made any secret about enjoying singing. So the fact that I've been able to spend a lot of my life putting the two together, has been a source of unending joy for me. I enjoy singing hymns, the majestic music that exalts Him and raises our sights and our spirits.'

Born in Bristol, Tennessee, on February 13, 1919, Ernest Jennings Ford, was bred upon country music and gained his basic groundwork, through listening to

country musicians, either in person or on the radio. His first entrance into show business came in 1937 with a local radio station – which he had been hanging around, and pestering the staff for a job, for quite a while – when he was hired as a staff announcer for 10 dollars a week.

Meanwhile, he was taking private singing lessons. He later went on to study voice at the Cincinnati Conservatory of Music. From 1939 to 1941 he was a radio announcer in Atlanta and Knoxville. When World War II broke out, Ernie enlisted in the Air Corps and flew heavy bombers as a bombardier. While stationed in California he met a young lady named Betty Heminger, wooed and married her. After the War, Ernie and Betty returned to Bristol. Things were tight there though, so the Fords bought an old car and headed west.

Ernie's first job on the West Coast was with a San Bernardino radio station, followed by a short stint as chief announcer for a station in Nevada. Ernie later returned to California where he became a hillbilly disc jockey for KXLA in Pasadena. Ernie's first day at the station turned out to be one of the most memorable of his life. Ernie recalls, 'I ran into the studio while Cliffie Stone's show was on the air, exchanged a few jokes, sang a hymn with the quartet, and left. It was just for fun – didn't pay a thing!' However, Cliffie insisted that Ernie join his Saturday night gang on the air as a regular. That was the beginning of the legendary 'Tennessee Ernie Ford'. In 1947, Capitol Records A & R man Lee Gillette heard Ernie one morning, singing along in that now-famous, deep and mellow voice with the record he was playing. 'The first thing I did when I got into the office was to call Cliffie at KXLA and tell him to bring that Tennessee Ernie fellow to me!' Cliffie recalls. 'In 1948 Placentia, California, was a small town not too far from what is now known as Disneyland. In the American Legion Hall, smack in the middle of an orange grove, I first introduced 'Tennessee Ernie' to the World. He came on stage bashfully, a dejected looking figure in his too-big bib-overalls, a checkered shirt, floppy hat, brogan shoes and a blacked-out tooth. With the opening lines of 'Mule Skinner Blues', Ernie took over that hall and that audience as he has done since with audiences all over the World. He and his wife, Betty, thought 25 dollars was too much to get paid for that appearance.'

With the appropriate contractual arrangements quickly dealt with and put to one side, Lee Gillette soon settled himself to producing Capitol's newest recording artiste. And the results were fast in coming through. In 1949 Tennessee Ernie struck home with two Top Ten Country successes, 'Mule Train' and 'Smokey Mountain Boogie', the latter being a number that he composed with Cliffie Stone. The following year, however, was to provide even greater successes with 'Anticipation Blues', 'I'll never be Free' (a duet with Kay Starr) and 'The Cry of the Wild Goose' all making the Top Ten whilst 'Shotgun Boogie', a Ford original, made the number one slot and collected a world-wide legion of fans.

The record sales added power to Tennessee Ernie Ford's name and, whilst such items as 'Mister and Mississippi', 'Blackberry Boogie' and 'The River of No Return' the theme from the Robert Mitchum/ Marilyn Monroe movie – maintained the array of chart listings, he proceeded to conquer fresh fields by becoming a major radio network figure by having his own shows on CBS and ABC during the period 1950–1955.

During the latter part of 1955 came 'Sixteen Tons' – and his biggest recording to date, as well as being the fastest selling record in Capitol's history at that time. 'Sixteen Tons' was written, and originally recorded by Merle Travis in 1947 as one of a selection of coal-mining songs, with the chorus – in particular the line 'I owe my soul to the company store' – being a saying that his coal-mining father had often used. Within three weeks it had sold one million copies, two million within nine weeks and by 1967, over 4,000,000 copies had been sold throughout the world markets.

When he achieved success, on radio, on television, on records, songs of faith and devotion were still a major part of his life. His show always ended with a hymn, and Ernie's albums of religious songs were always warmly received. On one occasion he commented, "All the masses of Atomic and Hydrogen Energy, Missiles and Satellites and Rockets are but a puff of wind when compared to the power of prayerful lyrics.'

From his boyhood days Tennessee Ernie remembers with warmth, 'One of the best things you can do with a song is bring comfort to people who need it. Some of the people who needed it most were the prisoners back there in the jails around Bristol, Tennessee. They needed a lot of things, cleanliness, decent food, punishments that fit their crimes, and so on. But their situation being as bad as it usually was, they sure needed some singing to brighten the corner where they were stuck.'

'I guess I was about ten or eleven when Dad brought a blind preacher home one day. A friend of his. And the idea was that we were all going down to a prison to put on a service and do some singing. It was out in the country, and the place we were taken to was a big, old, long, dirty building. Inside were rows of beds, close together, and an aisle down the middle. We stood around waiting a while and then we heard a shuffling and a clanking and in came the prisoners. They were right from the rock pile, a dusty lot, all chained together at the ankles. It was the first time I'd ever seen a real chain gang.'

'First we sang, my folks and I, and then the blind preacher took over. I forget what he said, of course, I was too busy staring all over the place, you know, the way a kid does. Those prisoners were a mighty sad lot, but the songs and the sermon seemed to reach them. They really seemed happier for us being there. It all must have added up to some kind of message of hope or solace. It did to us, and I think it did to them.'

'Another time I remember we sang in the Sullivan County Jail. It was during the Christmas season. We stood in the hall of this little jail and sang a whole bunch of songs, mostly Christmas songs. The men were back in their cells, and although they weren't as beat down as the chain gang bunch, they were just as sad and lonely and in need of some love and understanding.'

'After singing a while we stopped and passed out books and magazines and cigarettes that we'd brought along. Not all of the men were in cells; some of them were just standing around, I guess they were trusties. And it was one of those that caught my mother's eye. He was off in a corner, moping, looking real down. My mother went over to him and said, "Do we really sound that bad?" He didn't smile. he just said in a sort of dead voice, "No, but there ain't nobody can do anything for me. I killed a man." '

'Mother kept talking to him for a while, I think mainly to show him that she was interested in him, and she finally came around to the point she was trying to make. "Are you sorry you killed the man?" she asked, "or are you sorry you got caught? There's a difference, you know."

'They talked a little more, and before you knew it the man was even smiling. As she left, Mother said, "I don't know how long you're going to be here, but you can be forgiven. All you got to do is believe it."

'Then we had to leave. This is one of the times, however, when I was pretty sure that something good had come of our visit. I was pretty sure that my Mother had that day been serving man and God. Like it says in the Bible – "Inasmuch as ye have done it unto one of the least of these my brethren, ye have done it unto me." '

There were several fields into which he entered and soon found himself a master of. Television was but one and a guest slot on 'I love Lucy' brought about so much reaction that Lucille Ball had him brought back again for another appearance. The success of 'Sixteen Tons', naturally enough, brought about its own demands and by the end of 1955, Tennesse Ernie Ford was featured on his own daytime show on NBC-TV. Soon afterwards, brought about by even further enthusiastic audience response, he moved to a night-time slot.

Ernie Ford, had risen from a comparative unknown in the entertainment business to become one of the leading radio and TV recording artists in the World.

His devoted and straightforward singing of hymns highlighted his night-time television show for many years. These grand old songs, were ideally suited to his frank and engaging baritone.

In 1961 he turned away from television in order to devote more time to his wife and two sons, and the Fords moved from Los Angeles to a 540 acre ranch in the peninsular hills of San Francisco where he could fish and raise cattle to his heart's content!

After 25 years with Capitol records he turned his musical attention to the new songs that emanated from the 'Jesus Generation'.

About these new songs Ernie states; 'They clearly reflect the "new work" which is happening in Christian circles the world over – a passing away of traditional emphasis on denominational lines and a coming together in Jesus' Name for Christian Fellowship. The songs are not meant to be evangelistic but rather invitational by the warmth of their presentation. I call them "ministry songs" because they abundantly communicate the three great principals of Christian experience: *The Faith* we live by, *the Hope* we look for, and *the Love* we walk in. It is my sincere prayer that the listener receives from my songs the invitation to "enter into His courts with praise and thanksgiving". And join me in singleness of heart and make a joyful noise unto the Lord.'

This then is Ernie Ford; one of the world's most beloved and versatile entertainers whose unusual scope and talent have established him for more than a generation as a leading star in the pop, country and the religious fields of music.

There is probably not a single vocal genre he hasn't mastered. He's done pop tunes, folk, country, patriotic, Hawaiian – practically everything but the famous aria from 'Pagliacci' and if someone could get a microphone into Ernie's shower, you might get that too!

An example of his fidelity and staying power is his record of over 25 years with the same recording company. A score seldom achieved. To his millions of admirers he wrote, 'After twenty-five years with Capitol, what can I say? To be able to bring you these great Songs of Faith over the years has truly been a blessing in my life ... At this point in my life I feel very thankful and humble. It causes me to recall some words written years ago and found on the body of a fallen soldier during the War between the States. As you read them you will, I'm sure, understand my feelings ...'

I asked God for strength that I might achieve

I was made weak, that I might learn humbly to obey

I asked God for help, that I might do greater things

I was given infirmity, that I might do better things
I asked for riches, that I might be happy
I was given poverty, that I might be wise
I asked for all things, that I might enjoy life
I was given life, that I might enjoy all things
I was given nothing that I asked for
But everything I had hoped for
Despite myself, my prayers were answered
And I above all men am most richly blessed.

VII: Stuart Hamblen - 'The Beverly Hillbilly'

'The only thing I can ever give this World is Music' ... And how much richer the World is for the songs of Stuart Hamblen.

He was born on 20th October, 1908, the son of Rev. and Mrs. J. H. Hamblen in Kellyville, Texas. They had no indication that their baby was to grow into, without doubt, one of the most outstanding composers of Gospel Songs in the mid-20th century. Indeed, the years saw Stuart's life growing further and further away from the ideals of his godly parents' home. He spent his early life travelling the Lone Star State with his father – an itinerant preacher. Stuart loved the outdoor life; the freedom of the hills, plains, meadows and rivers. Between trips he studied at the McMurrey College in Abilene, preparing for a teaching career. As he worked his way through school he would take every opportunity to enjoy the outdoor skills of hunting and even bronco-busting which the young Stuart loved to practice. He developed an absorbing love of horses at this time, but a much more absorbing love was developing too – a love of music and singing. He loved to sing, often making up his own songs. Although he completed college and gained a degree in Education, he was always (in his own words) 'yearning to be places other than the classroom'. Music and the love of the outdoors had become his chief interests.

His first musical opportunity came after he won an amateur singing contest in Dallas, Texas. He was engaged to join a group of touring singers. Their tour led to California where he settled down. Later he joined the well-known 'Beverly Hillbillies' singing group of the late 1920's and early 1930's which included accordianist Zeke Manners and yodeller Elton Britt among its ranks. After hard years, success came and he became a much sought after solo Western entertainer on the Pacific coast. His radio programme ran for more than 20 years with great success. He also appeared in several Hollywood movies (usually as the 'bad guy'). This was the 'Golden Age of the Hollywood Cowboy'. Names such as Gene Autry, Roy Rogers, Tex Ritter and Rex Allen were becoming household names throughout the World. Stuart was right in the middle of all the excitement. Among his close friends were Western entertainers Roy Rogers and Dale Evans, Redd Harper, Bob Nolan, Tim Spencer, Wesley Tuttle and many others connected with the Western Film Industry and other branches of show business.

Beautiful songs just flowed from his pen and included such as 'Remember Me, I'm the One Who Loves You', (later to be recorded by such big-time stars as Elvis Presley, Johnny Cash and Pat Boone), 'This Ole House' (which became a world-wide 'pop' smash for Rosemary Clooney) and 'I won't go hunting with you Jake, But I'll go chasing women . . .' The sentiments expressed in the latter song, as one can tell from its title, gives some indication of the distance Stuart had moved from his parents' faith. A faith he never really had until a personal religious experience was to come to him.

Although very successful, he was, by his own admission, unhappy. One song he wrote which expressed his lack of happiness, joy, fulfilment, peace and purpose was

'Born to be happy – but always so sad,
Born to be good – but always so bad,
Born to be Somebody – yet fail in all I do
Born to be happy – but lost without You.'

In 1934 Stuart's 'Decca' label recording of 'Out on the Texas Plains' became one of the best selling discs of that year. During the 1930's many songs came from his pen including 'My Brown-eyed Texas Rose', 'Golden River', 'Just a little old rag doll' and the famous 'My Mary' (made famous by Jimmie Davis).

On 24th April 1933, he took his beautiful Suzy to be his wife. Suzy spent many hours praying for her husband during subsequent years. She knew his success was not bringing him peace and joy. She knew too, his love of hunting and horses were leading him deeper into the horse-racing life with all its moral pitfalls. Close acquaintances such as singers Redd Harper, Roy Rogers and Dale Evans and The Sons of the Pioneers were only too well aware of his quick and stormy temper. Despite the provocations Suzy was faithful in praying (often with tears) for her unhappy husband . . . And her answer was on the way.

In 1949 an unknown preacher from the hills of North Carolina was invited to conduct a city-wide campaign in Stuart's home town of Los Angeles. A huge tent – 'The Canvas Cathedral' – was pitched at the corner of Washington Boulevard and Hill Street and night after night it attracted thousands of men, women, and children. The message was not new – it was the evergreen Gospel of the crucified and risen Lord Jesus Christ; but the messenger was new – a young, unknown, blond, Southern Baptist bombshell by the name of Billy Graham!

Stuart was one of those who responded to the evangelist's invitation to make a decision for repentance, faith and total commitment to Jesus Christ. A decision that revolutionized his life. He announced his decision to the world dramatically on the next edition of his regular radio programme. The news caused a minor sensation in the newspapers and among the show business world of Hollywood and Los Angeles. The hard-living Stuart Hamblen, almost all said, was an unlikely candidate for conversion and 'How long will it last?' was the cynical question that circulated in a whisper among some . . . But it did last! Almost immediately he felt moral objections to the sponsor of his radio programme, because he felt he could no longer advertise the product concerned now he was a Christian. He sacrificed a programme he had retained for years and years.

Shortly after he had committed his life to Christ he is reported to have bumped into his friend, movie star John Wayne on a street in Los Angeles. John Wayne, aware of all the publicity that Stuart's conversion had attracted, enquired 'What's this I hear about you, Stuart?' 'Well, John,' came the answer, 'I guess it's no secret what God can do!' 'Sounds like a song,' the tall movie star remarked, and that remark started the thoughts and musical notes turning in Stuart's mind. They sent him to his home organ that night where the beautiful song 'It is no Secret' was born.

'It is no secret what God can do,
What He's done for others – He'll do for you.
With arms wide open – He'll pardon you,
It is no secret what God can do.'

Stuart recorded the song and between 20th Nov. 1950 and the end of the year the 'London' label released a cover of the song by Ray Smith and another by

Bob Houston and Jack Pleis; 'RCA Victor' followed with Elton Britt and The Three Suns; 'Mercury' cut with Ernie Lee and Kitty Kallen and Richard Hayes; and 'Columbia' rushed out discs by the Mariners, Jo Stafford and Stuart Hamblen himself. The following year 32 additional versions of the song appeared on the market. These included versions by many gospel and sacred singers such as George Beverly Shea, Blackwood Brothers, and Mahalia Jackson. The appeal of the song was so broad that it eventually appeared on about 200 recordings and it still being freshly recorded today.

Following his conversion Stuart dedicated his talents into the religious field and in the years to come beautiful songs came such as 'His Hands' (recorded by Eddy Arnold, Tennessee Ernie Ford etc.), 'Until Then' (recorded by Jimmie Davis, Ray Price etc.) 'Known only to Him' (Don Gibson, Elvis etc.). The list goes on and on.

A popular radio programme of Stuart's for many years was the 'Cowboy Church' from which came such unusual songs as 'Don't send them kids to Sunday School – Get out of bed and take 'em!'. A friend who worked on this programme for 12 years with Stuart was ex-Sons of the Pioneers member – Wesley Tuttle. Wesley says, 'I remember Stuart Hamblen, one of the greatest showmen I have ever known, putting his performing self aside on Sunday afternoons, and finding real joy in leading an audience of 500 people in singing the great Hymns of the Church.'

In 1952 his deep religious convictions brought pressure on his social conscience and led him to run for no less than the office of President of the USA on a prohibition ticket. History records his failure to attain the goal, but his enthusiasm and skills were still to be used and channelled into edifying social endeavours.

E

Only once in a long, long while does a truly great religious songwriter emerge. Stuart Hamblen is such a case. His meteoric success as a singer and songwriter has helped to make sacred-ballad history. The songs that came from the pen of Stuart Hamblen had their start in his heart. His new songs address Christ as a close friend, and sing His praise with moving conviction and joy. There is genuine personal impact for every listerner whether he seeks inspiration, encouragement, comfort, or a meaning to existence.

VIII: George Hamilton IV - 'The International Ambassador of Country Music'

The image of George Hamilton IV as an entertainer has been found very acceptable to millions outside his beloved North Carolina Homeland. 'Since we are all the sum total of our experiences,' George thoughtfully supposes, 'that means country, pop, rock, folk and rhythm and blues have all left their mark on me and I reckon my "style" today evolved from these different "trends" and "sounds" that I've grown up with and been exposed to. I've been lots of things, even a "Country folk singer", and I'm not one for labels but if you must, call me a Country singer . . . that's all I ever wanted to be! I'd just like to be as good as I can as a performer, a family man, a human being and I'd like to be known as a citizen of the World.'

George Hamilton IV's visits to the UK to record his series for BBC TV, have proved to be annual events as the viewing audiences rise in proportion to his popularity. It is not surprising that he is acknowledged as the 'International Ambassador of Country Music', because his success spans several continents. He has had the unique achievement of having three different TV series running simultaneously in the UK, the USA and Canada; indeed, he has achieved star status, not only in these bulwarks of Protestant civilization, but is now rising to a similar status across the continent of Europe – both sides of the Iron Curtain!

Early in 1973 the Ambassador of Country Music crossed the East-West frontier for appearances in Moscow and Prague for the express purpose of presenting American Country Music .. the first American artiste to do so. In Prague he had four concerts at the Ice

Sports Stadium and was 'knocked out' by the attend-
ances of more than 28,000, which included the Czech
Minister of Culture. On reflection George modestly
asserts, 'I would like to make it clear – it wasn't me the
people accepted, but the music. Country Music is
'People music' – the music of the people and that transcends the barriers.' Yet, surprisingly, his 'greatest thrill'
was to come . . . 'I attended church over there – the
Moravian Church and sang 'Amazing Grace' for them.
Now if you go to church there you have to pay the
price. The price could be that you or your children will
never be allowed to pursue a higher education. It was
interesting to me that they had never heard the song
before, but through the interpreter they *understood* the
words. I watched their faces as the interpreter told
them what 'Amazing Grace' meant and I saw their
faces light up! It was the greatest thrill I felt during
the whole trip; it was all a thrill, but that probably
was the greatest.'

From Prague, George went to Russia, and stayed in a
hotel overlooking Red Square where he could observe at
first hand the 'goose-stepping' Red Army. He attended
a reception given by the Minister of Culture and later
lectured on Country Music at the Moscow University.
Following the lecture he asked the students if they had
any comments and was surprised when instead he was
requested by a student to join them in a 'sing-a-long'.

'Chills ran all over me when they sang with me "This
land is Your Land", "When the Saints go marching in"
and others. They then sang a song for me that they
thought I wouldn't like. But instead of singing "We're
Gonna Lay Down Our Troubles Down By the Riverside", they sang "We're Gonna lay down Our Atom
Bombs Down by the Riverside" . . . it was something
else!' From his experience George concludes, 'This

69

whole trip just underscores something . . . Music is the common denominator!'

The amiable George Hamilton IV (his legal name) was born on 19th July 1937 in Winston-Salem, North Carolina, the fourth Hamilton named 'George'. 'I was raised in what they call the "Bible Belt". I don't know if people know what I mean by that expression, but it's a section of country back in the States that's *very* religiously orientated. The area has lots of churches and most people are actively involved in church activities. The way a person is brought up, the kind of atmosphere he lives in, and the way his parents think tends to rub off on him. I was raised in the Sunday School and Church atmosphere. My parents always insisted I go to Sunday School and they went with me! They didn't just send me down there!'

'We now have three children and we're all now very active in the Providence Baptist Church in Charlotte, North Carolina. My children sing in the choir, go to training union on Sunday nights and on Wednesday nights we all go to the Church supper, where we members of the Church get together for a fellowship supper followed by a devotional period with the Pastor.'

'I don't think it hurts to re-examine our traditions and beginnings in order to be more basic, down-to-earth and honest. Things are so complicated these days that we may forget there is elegance in simplicity.'

At the age of 12 George was permitted by his parents to take the long interstate bus ride all by himself from Winston-Salem to Nashville, Tennessee, to see the great stars of American Country Music in person. It was a schoolboy's fantasy come true and confirmed his ambition to enter the down-home arena of Country Music Show Business.

George was attending the University of North Carolina at Chapel Hill and was barely 19 years of age when his initial recording effort soared to sales of over one million copies. It was a silly little ditty entitled 'A Rose and Baby Ruth' – typical of 1957's teenage-love ballads. George thought little of the song. 'I laughed... I thought it was the corniest song I'd never heard.' But it set him on his way to, firstly, a contract with ABC Paramount and, secondly, international stardom.

In 1959 George and his wife, the former Adelaide Peyton (his childhood sweetheart) made the big move to Nashville, Tennessee – 'Music City USA'... the home of America's recording industry. The success that followed is popular music history and yet George has remained the unspoilt, down-to-earth country boy from the hills of North Carolina.

'I really believe in our World today, there are many people who are out on their own "ego trips". We hear so much of the 'I, I, I' and the 'me, me, me' all around us today. I heard an entertainer on the plane the other day who said, "You know, it's hard to communicate with other entertainers because they all want to star in their own movies." I think he was referring to this "me, me, me" and "I, I, I" in showbusiness; but it's all around us.'

Music today is giving the people poetry, theology and philosophy... and the music of George Hamilton IV is no exception. George affirms that, "I don't want to disappoint people or let them down. It's my duty and obligation to entertain, and I want to give folks their money's worth. But I want to get a message across. I want to paint a picture, tell a story.'

'Trends now just reflect the general feeling in the World today that things are getting pretty sick. The pornography in the movies and all the other dirt and filth around us is sickening. I think we're all beginning to react to that, and kinda wishing for a return to a time when things weren't so "Romanistic" or decadent. Most of us are fed up with all the emphasis on the seamier side of life and that's probably the reason people are turning back to deeper things. One of my favourite verses of scripture in the Bible is "Whatsoever things are good, whatsoever things are pure, whatsoever things are true – think on these things." '

'My biggest problem as a Christian in showbusiness is not so much *what* I believe but is being able to live up to what I believe in! It's one thing to believe something and to feel it very deeply, but it's something else to put it into daily practice. I have very deep convictions and beliefs which I feel very strongly about, but I don't pretend to be a saint. I've made mistakes, and still make them – all sorts of them – but the important thing, I think, is to realize that and not make a show . . . as an entertainer it's very easy to get into the dangerous trap of making a 'show' of religion. I don't say I'm a good person, yet – I'd like to be and I'm still trying to learn how. What we all need to do is to try harder to do what we already know is the right thing.'

'I moved back to North Carolina in August 1972 because I wanted to spend more time with my family. I loved Nashville, but the problem there was it seemed I was always "on the road". The little bit of time I was home and off the road it seemed was spent at the studio. Now in North Carolina I have cut down on my road-work and only work weekend dates. During the week I'm home with my family and working with my friend Arthur Smith on his syndicated TV Show.'

Arthur Smith, who provides the backing on George's two gospel albums 'Bluegrass Gospel' (Lamb and Lion) and 'Singing on the Mountain' (RCA) has made a deep impact on George. 'Arthur is a fine Christian man who has written some fine sacred songs such as "Acres of Diamonds" . . . "I saw a Man". The latter song has a lot to say I think is most important. "If I be lifted up, I will draw all men unto me" – that's the theme of the song, and it's a beautiful thought! A few years ago Arthur was voted the "Layman of the Year" by the Southern Baptist Convention, and is a very close friend of George Beverly Shea and Billy Graham.'

Close neighbours and friends of the Hamilton family is Billy Graham's brother-in-law Leighton Ford. George has a great respect and interest in Billy Graham, 'Billy was born near Charlotte where I live, and lives now in Montreat on top of a beautiful mountain in the Smokey Mountain range. He is, of course, greatly loved and respected in my part of the country, and being a Baptist I've heard of him all my life! I met him, very briefly, in Washington DC a couple of years ago at the Presidential Prayer Breakfast, which was not really a cosy little get-together with the President, because there were several hundred people from all over the country there. Ex-President Nixon was there and made a little speech, then he introduced the Reverend Graham, and Connie Smith sang. Billy afterwards met us briefly but he's a striking person to meet. He makes a lasting impression and I respect him very much.'

George has observed at first hand the renewed interest in Christianity among today's youth. 'The Jesus Revolution', I think, is a good thing. I know there is a lot of "fadism" and a lot of "jumping on the bandwagon" because it's the latest gimmick doing the rounds. If it is a gimmick it's a whole lot better than drugs and some of the other fads that have come along. Quite possibly these things the kids are studying in the Bible and discussing with their friends may rub off and stick! And

I suppose the people who are in it for fun and games, or for something trendy, will fade by the wayside, and those others who are sincere will have spiritual experiences that will last.'

The globe-trotting musical assignments of George IV have taken him from the USA to Canada, the UK, throughout Europe, Israel, Russia, Czechloslovakia – the list is almost inexhaustible, but he takes with his songs a message. At every stage appearance he makes, he endeavours to include a song of faith among the Country Music repertoire.

'One Gospel Song which is one of my favourites is, "Must Jesus Bear The Cross Alone?" When someone gives you a great gift, how can we smack him in the face? How can we return graciousness, or any gift in a bad way? After the things Jesus has done for us in the crucifixion . . . all the suffering and humiliation. How can we turn around and ignore Him? Not only not serve Him, but ignore Him!'

George Hamilton IV is a thinking artist who makes his audience think. All his songs are rich in imagery, have crisp lyrics, good feeling and content, and last, but not least – a message. 'As I understand the Christian ethic,' George thoughtfully observes, 'it is love and understanding and communication . . . brotherhood . . . that is, help for your fellow man is more important than laying up riches in the storehouse.'

IX: Redd Harper - 'Mr. Texas'

Redd Harper, author, singer, composer, and speaker in the fields of religion and music is called 'Mr. Texas' by hundreds of thousands of followers because he played that role in the film of the same name.

They call him 'Mr. Texas' but he belongs to the entire World. He was born in the Lone Star State – Nocona, Texas to be precise – on 29th September 1903. He was raised however, in the beautiful, wide-open ranges of Oklahoma where most of his early life was spent in the saddle. Instead of becoming a cowhand or a cattleman he entered the University of Oklahoma. 'I had most of my schooling in a town called Muskogee – of course, there's been a big song out by Merle Haggard called the 'Okie from Muskogee' . . . You might call me the 'Texan from Muskogee', Redd recalls.

After his studies at the University of Oklahoma he had a short spell as a newspaper reporter. Later he was invited to join a dance band which soon became very successful and eventually landed Redd with a great deal of radio work at Radio Station WKY in Oklahoma City from 1924–5 and stations KSO and KRNT in Des Moines (1931–3). This success eventually led him to the then 'Entertainment Capital of the World' – Hollywood.

Redd reminisces, 'I went out to set the World on fire but it wasn't long before them people in Hollywood put the fire out! . . . I went to work in a night club with a

western band led by Jimmy Greer that was very big in those days. The show was called "The Musical Host of the Coast" and we played all the big parties for the movie stars including the famous Academy Award Dinners.'

Just before World War II broke out Redd went back into radio – writing and producing a programme for the Mutual Network. However the war interrupted things and Uncle Sam required his services for three years. 'After that I had to start all over again.'

Well, the success he had worked for and deserved eventually came. He originated and produced a series of very successful radio programmes entitled 'Redd Harper's Hollywood Roundup' (from 1945–50). Redd continues, 'It was the sort of a western Hedda Hopper or Louella Parsons . . . I'd have the news from the western field and had as guests the people (who were in radio, rodeo, TV and movies) who I then interviewed. If they were singing stars – naturally I would have them sing some songs on the programme. If it was an action movie cowboy, well, we'd play a little scene from the sound-track of his latest movie.' Guests included Eddy Arnold, Tennessee Ernie Ford, Roy Acuff, Ernest Tubb, Hank Snow, Hank Thompson, Rex Allen, Bob Wills, Johnny Bond, Merle Travis, and Tex Ritter.

His close acquaintances included Roy Rogers and Dale Evans, the Sons of the Pioneers, and also the great western singer-songwriter-performer Stuart Hamblen.

'When I first went to Hollywood in 1932 I worked for Stuart Hamblen . . . and he fired me! . . . And I hated him! . . . Well, he was a drunkard – he drank all of the time. He came to work one night at the American Legion Stadium at Southgate and I was singing a song. All the people had stopped dancing and were listening to me sing. He couldn't take that, no sir, he didn't like it and fired me! Well, I kinda hated him but you know a person like him you had to tolerate because he was so popular. He had one of the most popular programmes ever to hit Hollywood.

. . . . He'd sing all religious music – that's what the country and western fans liked. (By the way – every programme I ever had, I'd always close with a religious song.) But Stuart would also give some homespun talk, kinda semi-religious. I would often join him as a guest and while the quartet were on stage singing he'd say "Come on Harp, let's go round the back." He'd grab a bottle and we'd take a slug a' bourbon outa it in turn . . . then I'd go out and take a hymn book and sing some song like "The Old Rugged Cross" but I didn't know then what I was singing about – I'd never been to Calvary – never realized that Jesus Christ died on that Old Rugged Cross for me personally . . . Later I heard that Stuart had been converted and got religion. I laughed about it and said to myself "Oh, that big phony!" He's just putting that on. Then they told me he'd quit the radio and gone out as an evangelist and I said, "Well, if he's doing that he's making more money then he did on the radio!" But Buddy Dooley who was playing bass with Stuart told me, "Well, I don't know how many preachers you know who earn 2,000 dollars a week like Stuart had been earning." That kinda stumped me a little. Then one night I went to this Hollywood Christian Group where Stuart gave his testimony. I realized that night that he wasn't the same man I used to work for. Later on when I received Christ as Saviour and this change happened to me I realized what had happened to Stuart. After my conversion the first person I looked up was Stuart Hamblen.'

It was through attendance at the Hollywood Christian Group in 1950 that Redd had this religious experience. Roy Rogers – the President of the Group – says of Redd's experience, 'I have seen first hand the emergence of the soul of Redd Harper from darkness into stimulating Christian experience.' And Dale Evans adds, 'I personally knew Redd BC and AC (Before and After Conversion), and his message is amazing.' The gracious husband and wife duo witnessed the tremendous transformation. About

Roy and Dale, Redd recalls, 'I have known Roy and Dale for many years now, I knew them even before they knew each other! I knew Roy when he was just plain Len Slye – the lead singer, guitar picker and best yodeller of the Sons of the Pioneers. And Dale was the guest on my pilot show "Redd Harper's Hollywood Roundup". They have remained dear, close friends of my wife and I for many, many years.'

Redd soon realized what his songs, music and writing talents could accomplish for the promotion of his faith. He always says, 'God made a songwriter outa me' because he denies any natural talent in that direction. Many great favourites have flowed from his pen which have been recorded by many great artists such as Tommy Collins, Jimmy Swaggart, Tony Fontaine, Cliff Barrows, Roy Rogers and Dale Evans, Alan McGill, George Beverly Shea and many more. Also in collaboration with Dr. Oswald J. Smith, the famed pastor and missionary statesman of Peoples Church, Toronto, Canada, he composed many gospel classics. Redd's records have sold in their thousands on the Capitol, Decca Emerald, Sacred, Christian Faith and Word labels. In 1954 he was presented with the coveted ASCAP Award for his songwriting talents.

Chosen to play the role of 'Mr. Texas' in the film of the same name, Redd has been called 'Mr. Texas' ever since. He later appeared in 'Oiltown USA' and in the early sixties in two films entitled 'The Gospel according to some people' and 'God loves people'. Cindy Walker, the renowned country music songwriter was chosen in the co-starring role with Redd in both 'Mr. Texas' and 'Oiltown USA'.

For three years following his conversion Redd travelled extensively with the Billy Graham Party that included George Beverly Shea and Cliff Barrows. As a member of that team in 1954 he held three months of successful meetings in many areas of the British Isles including the famous meetings at Harringey Arena.

After three years as a member of the Billy Graham Team, Redd launched out on his own Evangelistic meetings, singing and telling his thrilling testimony of what the Lord had done for him. He made several missionary journeys to the South Pacific, New Zealand, Australia, The Phillipines, Hong Kong, Japan, Europe, Africa ... the list goes on and on. Yes, Texas takes first claim on Redd Harper but he belongs to the Whole World!

He makes his home in Hollywood with his wife but is now on the road most of the time in evangelistic work, singing and telling his thrilling story. A simple yet effective cowboy preacher he uses his guitar and his songs to help convey the gospel message.

X: Wanda Jackson - 'The Yodelling Sweetheart'

'Vivacious and versatile' – 'Talented and terrific' – are the adjectives to describe the artistry of pretty Wanda Jackson, a veteran star of Country Music, who has been singing and entertaining fans of Country Music throughout the World since her early teens.

Aside from being a great favourite of country music shows, fairs, rodeos, and all types of presentations all across the United States and Canada, Wanda is one of the few country music artists who has been so talented as to record her songs in native languages in both Germany and Japan. In 1971 she was voted 'The Favourite Country Music Singer' of the Scandinavian countries – Norway, Sweden, Denmark etc., and just a few years before had received a tremendous reception from country music fans in Japan, Phillipines, Korea and the Far East. In 1972 she did a tour of Australia, New Zealand and Japan, where a triumphant reception was received.

But today something is different . . . her voice is lighter . . . her face is happier . . . and her songs have a new, recurring theme . . . JESUS!

Wanda Jackson was born on a cold, October day of 1937 in a little community, tucked into the mid-Western state of Oklahoma, called Maud. When she was six-years-old economic necessity precipitated her family's move to the apparent prosperity of California. Tom Jackson, her father, was a part-time piano player in

local bands and a part-time worker in any other occupation that became available! War had broken out and greener pastures flickered in the minds of the Jacksons as they left the dust of their home state and headed to the booming West coast.

The family stayed in Los Angeles for three months,

during which time Tom Jackson learnt the barber's trade, but prosperity was still elusive so the family moved to Bakersfield. There they settled quickly into the friendly company of fellow 'Okies' from their home state. This common heritage and their country music traditions became the bonding factors that influenced the young, six-year-old Wanda. Soon she was joining in the home-spun entertainment – singing, playing guitar and reading music.

After the war the elusive dream of prosperity was still just as elusive to the Jacksons so they moved back home to Oklahoma, settling in Oklahoma City. Wanda's natural and attractive talent was becoming obvious, and she was persuaded to enter a talent contest. Her success in the contest secured her a daily, 15 minute radio programme. The time was very quickly extended to 30 minutes and attracted a high degree of popularity and attention throughout Oklahoma.

In 1954, Wanda Jackson caught the attention of one of the top singers and band leaders of that period – Hank Thompson. He was so impressed with her talent that he invited her to join his band as resident vocalist. Regular engagements with Hank Thompson's Brazos Valley Boys were soon followed by offers of record contracts. Decca won the race for her signature and recorded several discs that rose into the American Country Music Top Ten Charts. But even the limelight of success did not provide Wanda with the fulfilment she pursued.

Following her graduation from Capital Hill High School she continued her rise to fame. The Rock n' Roll bubble was beginning to expand commercially and she was lined up for tours alongside another rising star, Elvis Presley. A more acceptable record contract beckoned in 1956 from Capitol which Wanda enthu-

83

siastically received. Capitol were delighted with their new acquisition, especially when her discs started pounding the hit parades on both sides of the Atlantic. In particular, 'Let's Have a Party' climbed well into Britain's Top Ten back in 1958.

With her fame came the riches associated with it. By the sixties, although the Rock n' Roll bubble had burst, she was by then a well-established star in the consistent, secure World of Country Music. Fulfilment still eluded her. She had known little of a real home life because her numerous appearances kept her on the road for months at a time but in 1961 she married her manager, Wendell Goodman.

National acclaim was followed by international acclaim following successful discs and tours of Britain, Germany, Holland and Japan. She had made several big hits on the Continent with recordings made in foreign languages.

Twice Wanda has been nominated for Country Music's Oscar, the Grammy, for her single 'A woman lives for love' and for her album 'Two sides of Wanda'.

She was also chosen to sing on the first live 'Grammy Awards Show'. For five years she appeared with the late Red Foley on his 'Ozark Jubilee' and was a regular guest on the 'Dick Clark Show', a show which led to her popularity on the pop and rock fields as well as in the country music world.

Almost everything anyone could have desired had happened to Wanda . . . a popular performing artist at home and abroad . . . many hit records . . . fame . . . travel . . . riches . . . and much more! But still something was missing, . . . real fulfilment, happiness, joy and peace eluded her . . . until she found 'New Life in Jesus'. Her friend and pastor joyfully declares that today 'Wanda Jackson is a new person; as any of her friends can tell you!'

Wanda remembers, 'I'd joined the church when I was 13 – the same year that I got my first guitar – but I didn't understand what Salvation was. Then after my marriage, Wendell and I had no time or thought for God, although we did see to it that Mother kept our kids in Sunday School.'

Finally her pastor, Rev. Paul Salyer, reached Wanda and Wendell. 'We had lunch together . . . He didn't hit us over the head with a Bible or tell us that fire and brimstone were about to fall on us. He simply asked us if we wouldn't consider the abundant life that Christ wanted to give us,' Wendell remembered.

Three weeks later, after a conviction-packed Alaskan tour, the Goodmans committed their lives to Jesus Christ.

'Even before then, our house was like a three-ring circus,' Wanda said. 'But now, there's a new kind of excitement around, almost as though we're waiting to find a miracle around every corner.'

Most of the excitement is generated by the Romans 8:28 concept. 'So many folks apply this verse just to BIG THINGS in their lieves, but we know that nothing that happens to the Christian is insignificant,' Wanda explained. Wendell added, *'WE FEEL THAT CHRISTIANITY IS NOT A WAY OF LOOKING AT CERTAIN THINGS BUT A CERTAIN WAY OF LOOKING AT ALL THINGS!'*

Wanda also says that God puts her at the right place at the right time. At Easter 1972, Wanda performed in Rapid City, South Dakota. The 15-year-old daughter of the local bandleader confided that she was reluctantly considering the nightclub circuit. Wanda knew the problems and pitfalls of the amateur nightclub singer – one-night stands, smokey rooms, liquor-filled patrons, who shouted lewd things to the singer.

'I soon discovered that Michelle had a basic problem greater than the nightclub decision. Her heart was hungry for the Lord, so I showed her how to give her heart to Jesus,' Wanda said.

By the next Easter, Michelle's sister and mother had been converted to Christ. A few weeks later Wanda returned to Rapid City – without her luggage and the tape equipment for her performance – which didn't arrive until after she did. 'God had a hand in this too, though ... I swallowed my pride, accompanied myself at the piano and prayed while Wendell gave his testimony in the little Church.'

When the invitation was given, Michelle's father (who had come only because he was a Wanda Jackson fan) and her brother were the first at the altar. However, the chain of conversions began because Wanda was in the right place at the right time to lead Michelle to Christ.

The new Wanda Jackson has found fulfilment in personal faith in Jesus Christ and consequently takes all available opportunities to give her testimony of what God has done for her. During the nearly twenty years she had spent with Capitol she had never recorded a religious album, unlike most country singers. When asked about this she truthfully replied, 'How could I sing about a person that I did not really know?' Almost immediately after her conversion she recorded her first religious album. She now knows the One she is singing about!

Not content with the Christian opportunities offered by Capitol, she left them and surprised everyone by signing for the Christian-based 'Word Record Company'. Obviously she treasured to a much greater degree her Christian testimony and witness above the retention of a very financially rewarding top, secular, recording contract.

Wanda and Wendell gladly tell all whom they meet today that things are now different. Christ has given them a joy and certainty that comes from believing that they intend to share with anyone who listens.

XI- Roy Rogers and Dale Evans—
The King of the Cowboys and the
Queen of the West

The mention of the names Roy Rogers and Dale Evans makes nostalgia overflow from the hearts of thousands who still preserve a special place for this husband and wife duo. These days Roy and Dale make their home on their sprawling Double-R Ranch in Apple Valley, Southern California. In many ways this pleasant, friendly, and happy couple are really quite unlike most people who owe their success to the harsh 'dog-eat-dog' world of showbusiness. Despite that association they are known and loved by kids and grown-ups everywhere. They have truly remained unspoilt, down-to-earth folk. Their neighbourhood in Chatsworth – a charming community in the San Fernando Valley, know this couple not as 'snobbish' show-biz personalities but as dedicated parents and active workers in both church and civic affairs. Indeed, Roy served his community as Mayor for many years.

Roy's rise to world-wide fame brought him the title 'King of the Cowboys' through the medium of his ninety feature-length movies which helped brighten a saddened, war-sick globe in the decade that followed World War II. In addition, with his attractive wife Dale, he delighted millions more with the tremendously popular TV series.

He was born Leonard Slye on a cold November day in 1912 and was raised on a farm in the rural community

of Duck Run, Ohio. His boyhood home was a traditional little 'clap-board' house in the hills. It was built by Roy when he was eleven with perhaps more than a little help from his father. During these years he found it easy to pick up the mandolin and guitar because both his parents were good musicians. They played regularly for square-dances and socials on Saturday nights. At high school Roy's contemporaries were a wild, rough bunch. Among such company he almost landed himself in re-form school. He loved the country way of life and became an expert farm-boy. One year his expertize won him the prize at the Scioto County Fair for his big, fat sow. The winnings was an all-expenses-paid trip to the big city for a week. The big city was, in fact, the State Capital – Columbus, Ohio. The excited Slye youngster could not get over the store lifts and spent a considerable amount of those days riding up and down!

With schooldays done, Roy and his parents headed towards California with thousands of others trying to escape the famines of the 1930's Great Depression. Roy (or Len, as he was then known) was willing to take any job to keep the family table supplied. His subsequent occupations included shoe-making, road-building and house painting. He even drove a sand and gravel truck for a while but his employer 'went bust' . . . and so did Roy's job. He headed north to the San Joaquin Valley and picked peaches in the orchards of the Del Monte Packing Company. These were tight, lean years for the family but Roy loved them and is grateful for them.

Without a good foundation of education, Roy had to learn as he went along – it was the hard way and the most rewarding. When the peach-picking season ended there was no work to be found for the unskilled . . . so Roy joined the unemployed. He started to concentrate and develop his singing and mandolin playing and formed a group called 'The Rocky Mountaineers'. Soon radio opportunities followed. Changing his name from Len Slye to Dick Weston, he helped form the famous cowboy singing group – 'The Sons of the Pioneers' who were often used in director John Ford's movies. Originally a trio, the group became famous for their yodelling in three-part harmony. So, Roy's show biz career began to blossom and in 1937 he signed for Republic Studios. Very shrewdly he spent a year on a Montana ranch and learned the arts and crafts of riding and shooting.

The top singing cowboy of the day was Gene Autry but from Roy's first starring-role in 'Under Western Skies' it was obvious that a brighter star was rising. Soon he had the field to himself and the billing 'The King of the Cowboys'. The action-filled musical extravaganzas set in the West showed Roy and his wife Dale immaculately dressed in extremely ornate cowboy costumes. In addition, they owned the most famous animal movie-star 'Trigger – the smartest horse in the movies'. Throughout the world, toys, books, clothes, etc., began to appear bearing the Roy Rogers brand tag as numerous companies cashed in on this successful Hollywood image. After the movie success came hundreds of television, radio and rodeo dates.

On the personal side, Roy lost his first wife Grace Arlene when their baby was born in 1946. Later he married his co-star of earlier years – Dale Evans.

The conversion of Roy and Dale is familiar to many people but it's good enough to bear repeating.

Tom, whose father had passed on, was Dale's son by her first marriage. One Sunday evening he invited his Mother to attend church with him at the Fountain Avenue Baptist Church, Los Angeles. Tom's girl friend

91

and soon-to-be-wife was the organist there, and Dr. Jack MacArthur was the pastor. During the invitation Tom asked, 'Mother, is everything all right between you and the Lord?' 'Why, certainly!' she snapped. 'I was baptized, and I joined the church when I was ten years old.'

But in her heart Dale knew she was far, far from the Lord. It really broke her up inside when Tom said: 'You sure don't act much like a Christian, Mother.'

Dale brooded over this all week under deep conviction, and the following Sunday found her going forward and committing her life afresh to the Lord.

Roy saw the change in his wife immediately; as a matter of fact, the whole Roger's household was aware of the presence of Christ in Dale Evans. She started prayers at every meal and daily reading of the Word of God with the family. Roy finally decided to go to church with them. Dale and the kids were so happy that he thought he ought to try it too.

At one service during the invitation Dale asked Roy, 'Wouldn't you like to go forward and give your heart to Christ?' 'No!' Roy whispered hoarsely. 'And don't ask me that again – ever!'

Dale was hurt and disappointed, but she hoped and prayed she had not spoiled everything. On the way home Roy explained, 'Look honey – if I ever go forward at church, I want to be sure it's of God and not of anyone else.'

Not too many Sundays later, of his own accord, and without a word to anyone, Roy got up from his seat in the balcony and walked down the stairs and down the aisle to give his heart and life to the Lord Jesus. Rev. Noel Lyons counselled Roy in the inquiry room. It caused quite a stir in the Church. So much so that the minister offered to have a private baptismal service just for him. 'No siree,' Roy insisted, 'I'll be baptized just like everyone else.' . . . And he was.

It was not long until the news of their conversions became the sensation of Hollywood and the amazement of their many friends.

Redd Harper recalls a visit he paid to the Rogers home, before his own conversion and about a month after theirs. 'My wife and I had been somewhere with Roy and Dale and they invited us home with them as the evening was still fairly young. But instead of leading us down to the trophy room with its bar, they led the way to the kitchen, where we sat down in their breakfast nook.

'Shall I put on a pot of coffee, or would you just as soon have a coke or ginger ale?" Dale asked us. I shrugged a "makes no difference to me," but I guess they both saw the wonderment in my eyes. "I suppose you are wondering why we aren't offering you something stronger to drink, huh?" asked Roy. "Why, no," I lied, thinking that surely they hadn't become so religious they wouldn't even offer a friend a "night cap". "Well, it's this way," they hastened to explain. "When we received Christ as our Saviour, why, we just turned over our lives and everything to Him. Our home, the kids – everything!'

Through the years Roy and Dale have had their share of family tragedy. Their only natural child (from *their* marriage) was born handicapped and disabled, and died when she was only two. They lost their teenage-boy Sandy – who died in Germany serving in the US Army. One of their adopted children – a little Korean girl named Debbie – was killed in a church-bus motorway accident when she was only eleven.

No, their thirty years of marriage have not been without their trials and tragedies yet despite such personal loss their optimistic faith, courage, and energetic involvement in evangelistic endeavours have been a source of inspiration to people everywhere. Their home, family, and personalities reflect their steadfast faith and belief in the power of prayer. No 'in-person' appearance by Roy or Dale ever fails to include one song of faith. Their involvement with evangelistic endeavours really began in England. In 1954 they joined Dr. Billy Graham for the historic Harringey meetings.

Despite the trials and tribulations of the years Dale adamantly states, '*God is a good God!* The indescribable joy He has let me experience in the Spirit far transcends any trials He has let me experience. The joy He has given in allowing me to work out my own salvation in fear and trembling – well, I wouldn't trade that for anything the World has to offer. The fact that He has permitted me to see each one of the children, and Roy, accept Jesus Christ means that he has been far more than fair with me. The tears He has allowed to dim the eyes of my flesh have cleared the eyes of my soul, bringing each time a new depth of spiritual understanding and vision – because I trust Him.'

XII: Connie Smith - 'The Gal with the Big Voice'

'You know, I never wanted to be a singer. I wanted to sing, but I didn't want to be a singer! Even now, my greatest job – and the one I like best – is being a mamma . . .'

Well, even if she didn't want it – still Connie Smith has emerged from the crowded corridors of would-be stars into the spotlight of Nashville's musical elite. What did she possess that gave her the advantage over the many other thousands seeking fame? George Jones, another of Nashville's Super Stars has no doubt that it was 'soul'. Declares George, ' "Soul" is a word that we in the business of making country music identify with a certain feeling. It's an intangible item but you can sense when it's there, and, believe me, it's in the great singing of Connie Smith. In music, Connie's everything she is as a human being: a sincere person with a big heart and a lot of soul, and I'm mighty proud to be her friend.'

How she was signed to an exclusive RCA Victor contract by Chet Atkins and had a smash hit with her first single, 'Once a Day', is what might well be called a modern Cinderella story, Nashville style.

What events led Connie Smith from Elkhart, Indiana via southern Ohio to Nashville, Tennessee where she became one of the most respected and admired talents in country music? 'Things just happened,' she said, 'I never

really planned to be a singer. My family moved from Indiana to south eastern Ohio when I was 10 years old and I call Warner, Ohio, my home town. I was kind of quiet as a child, but I used to sing some. I came from a very large family. My mother and father had five children, and after my father died, my mother married my stepfather who had eight, then they had one, so, altogether there were 14 kids!'

'I started singing in high school and after that I sang at PTA's, grange halls, electric company meetings, square dances, just about everywhere I guess.' One hot sunny day Connie sang at a country fair and a group from WSAZ TV station in Huntington, West Virginia heard her. They needed some local talent for their Saturday Night Jamboree, and Connie was their choice.

'I sang in Huntington for about nine months, and after that I didn't do any singing for a while.' However, a few months later Connie heard that George Jones was going to appear at a park in Columbus, Ohio. 'I had never seen a real live Grand Ole Opry star before,' she said, 'So my husband and I went up to see the show. It wasn't George though, it was Bill Anderson, but we were still happy about it because we liked Bill too. Then my husband talked me into entering a talent show, which I did – but there was a seven-year-old boy playing a banjo – and I thought nobody can win over that – but I did. Still, I think it was because the boy had been in so many contests and won so many that they just felt sorry for me and let me win that time.'

Modesty aside, Bill Anderson knew talent when he saw it. This was a turning point for Connie. He encouraged her to think of making a career in the music business.

'A few months later Bill was in Canton,' she recalls, 'and my husband and I went to see him there and he took us out to dinner and we talked some more about my singing and the business. Then he asked if I liked the business so much why I didn't come to Nashville. I said, "Oh, just like that, come to Nashville . . . I could never make it in Nashville . . ."

G

But she did with Bill's help. And how he helped! He brought her to Nashville in the spring of '64 and taped a dub with her. Then he had to go to Minnesota for a date at the 'Flame' and Connie went back to Ohio with apprehension and a feeling that nothing would happen. Then she found out that an agent had walked out of his talent agency with a tape that Bill had left him and headed for Chet Atkin's Office a block away to let the great guitarist and A & R man listen to the new sounds. Back Connie went to Nashville to put her name on the dotted line. Then Chet recorded 'Once a Day' in August 1964 and by October, it was Number One. She was Nashville's 'new sensation – 'the little gal with the big voice'.

Dallas Frazier, one of Nashville's top singer/songwriters remembered the time he first saw Connie Smith in person, 'I dropped by a recording session at RCA's Nashville studios and through the control-booth window I saw a very pretty girl with a beautiful voice. At the time, this pretty girl was singing a song about loving a fellow named Charley Brown. This particular songstress is, in my opinion, the greatest female country vocalist that has happened in the music industry in years. Speaking as a songwriter, I must tell you it's a rare occasion for any of us to hear his material "souled out" the way I was hearing it that day.'

Connie Smith's initial RCA Victor recording, 'Once a Day' occupied first place on the USA's country music best-seller charts for nearly two months late in 1964. On the basis of this hit, she was signed to make her national TV 'bow' on a Jimmy Dean Special, but the show was pre-empted twice: once because of the presidential campaign, later because of Thanksgiving. By the time the programme was finally aired in April, 1965, Connie's second record, 'Tiny Blue Transistor Radio', and her third, 'I can't Remember', were already among the top sellers.

On June 13, 1965, Connie became the first Hoosier to be named a Grand Ole Opry star in more than twenty years. In addition to her regular 'Opry' appearances, she has starred on the WGN 'Barn Dance', 'Swingin' Country', and 'The Lawrence Welk Show'. She has also made a number of films; 'Road to Nashville', 'Las Vegas Hillbillies', and 'Second Fiddle to an Old Steel Guitar'. In addition to her Cashbox and Record World honours of 1966, she received the International Western Market Pioneer Award as 'Best Vocalist, Country and Western Field'. The year before, she had been dubbed 'Most Promising Country Female Singer' by Billboard, Cashbox, and Country Music Review. The fact that makes these awards noteworthy is that only one year earlier she was just a housewife and mother in Warner, Ohio.

Despite all the travel and all the fun Connie admits freely that 'there were moments of feeling all alone and there was no special goal in life'. She had not found real fulfilment in fame and fortune. Finally, she found what had long eluded her – a relevant faith in a living, loving and personal Saviour. It happened after a period of deep searching. 'The Spirit of God was dealing with my heart,' she recalls. Finally she very simply gave her heart to the Lord Jesus in a TV Studio and was counselled by the Rev. Jimmie Snow, son of Hank Snow, and Pastor of Nashville's Evangel Temple Church.

It was not long before Connie was boldly speaking, without hesitation about her personal relationship with her Saviour. Her stand for God has caused unkind comments to be said about her which she is well aware of. 'I've had people say I'm just a fanatic . . . that I'll soon "burn out" and even that it's just an act . . . But you know – the same people who talk about me come to me when they are in trouble – not because they think I'm good, or that I can do anything, but they come, I hope, because they see Christ in me. I'm grateful for this, I don't know why God picked me to do His work, except that the Bible says that He picks the most foolish ... maybe that says it ... Of all the people in this business, I think I am the most unlikely! '

Not all her fellow artistes feel unkindly disposed to Connie's out-spoken expression of her deep inward Faith. Conway Twitty, reflecting on a week's visit Connie made to him ,his wife and family, says, 'We learned to enjoy the sweet and gentle person of Connie Smith as the week went on. Connie uses each day to effect a divine improvement of her inner self. We *felt* her faith in a higher power.'

Connie obviously is not backward in realizing the use she can put her singing talents to. She has consequently sang at evangelistic rallies throughout the USA with evangelists such as Billy Graham, David Wilkerson, and Bob Harrington. In addition, her natural talent has found magnificent self-expression of her faith in the recording studio. A gospel recording session with Connie Smith is always something special.

Bob Benson recalls with much appreciation his surprise when he first attended Connie Smith's first gospel recording session. Despite the fact that he had spent so many long hours in other Gospel Music recording sessions he discovered a freshness that made Connie's session come alive.

'I have spent a lot of time at gospel recording sessions, so I was quite anxious to see and hear this talented young artist from the country field doing gospel sessions at RCA Victor's Nashville Studio. When I arrived, the studio was crowded with musicians – pianist, organist, bass fiddler, drummer, vibes man, guitar players and Jake Hess and the Imperial Quartet. Chuck Seitz was at the engineering controls and Bob Ferguson in the producer's chair. The smallest person in the studio was the singer, Connie Smith. The usual improvization, spot arranging and tape preparations were in progress. When things got rolling a lot was going on – background voices; rhythm by bass, drums, guitar, fills by piano, guitars, vibes – *but suddenly Connie was the tallest person there!* It was hard to see where that big voice was coming from but it sure explained why she was "discovered" and why her singles and albums have been top sellers. Music demands sincerity and conviction, and all singers who become popular have an ability to feel and project the heart of a song. It seems that this is particularly true of gospel music, for it has a moral – a message to convey. The little girl with the big voice was more than a match for the task.'

Connie now freely states that her greatest thrill is to serve her Lord. 'I worry a lot more about doing God's work than my own,' she said, 'and I work a lot harder preparing for Gospel performances than my regular shows – just ask the guys who play music for me!'

XIII: Marijohn Wilkin - 'The Den Mother of Nashville'

Marijohn Wilkin could aptly be described as one of the 'myth-makers' of Nashville and her name ranked among the likes of Chet Atkins and Anita Kerr. She is a lady of so many diverse talents that it is very difficult to know exactly where to begin. In the UK it is probably by her song-writing talents that she is best known especially to the country and folk fans. 'Long Black Veil' (recorded by Johnny Cash, Joan Baez etc.), written by Marijohn, is an example of her undoubted songwriting talents. When asked about the most popular of her songs she replied, 'Well, of course 'Waterloo' (recorded by Stonewall Jackson) was the biggest as far as sellers are concerned. I wrote it with John D. Loudermilk. Also there was 'PT109' the story of John F. Kennedy's war exploits which was a big smash hit for Jimmie Dean.'

For the first six years that Marijohn lived in Nashville she wrote for the Cedarwood Publishing Company who accumulated a catalogue of over 300 of her songs. 'In those days we were told to go in and write for a certain artist; or write a ballad for "so and so"; or write an uptempo for "so and so". There were six writers, including Marijohn, who was assigned to these projects – John D. Loudermilk, Mel Tillis, Wayne Walker were among their ranks. If one of them had an idea for a song then one of the others would help them finish it. Most of this type of co-writing ceased in Nashville with the

advent of the singer-songwriter in the late sixties and early seventies.

During those Nashville years Marijohn was one of Nashville's most popular personalities. She even gained the name of 'Den Mother of Nashville' because of the way she was so quick to help young people financially. On several occcassions at great sacrifice to herself she willingly provided needy young people with a place to stay. She was also active in helping them get a break into the Music Scene.

That period of her life won her no less than eight BMI awards from the Music Industry for her songwriting achievements. She modestly asserts, however: 'as a songwriter I haven't done too well. That number of awards isn't a lot compared with some of the really great writers of Nashville.' Despite her modesty – eight awards is certainly not bad going!

At the end of those six years in which she was engrossed in her most commercial writing she started her own publishing company. This took time away from her own writing but during that time she formed and managed a vocal back-up group called 'The Marijohn Singers'. Her group was responsible for the vocal back-up on literally hundreds of Nashville Studio recordings. In addition she squeezed in time for the Singers to do a three year stint on the 'Grand Ole Opry TV Show' series.

As if all this creative work was not sufficient it is now widely known that Marijohn had more than a little to do with Kris Kristofferson getting his much needed early breaks. She recalls, 'Kris was stationed in the Services in Germany with a second cousin of mine – a young kid I hadn't seen in years. They were both from Texas so they had a kinda' mutual feeling for each other. And both were captains and helicopter pilots. Kris was already a sorta' renegade even at that time because he was a captain and yet he was playing with a non-commissioned music group in the NCO clubs. That scene was looked down upon by his fellow officers.'

'He sent me a tape from Germany with some of his first attempts at Country writing. He always had a love for music; even when he had been in school at Oxford, England he was recording. But when I got that tape I thought what a horrible voice . . . ha . . . ha . . . and yet it turned out to be good!'

'Later on in 1965 I remember Kris walked into my office . . . He had his hair cut short and his captain's uniform on. With his shoulders back he looked down at me and he said, "Are you Marijohn?" I said, "Yes – and you must be Captain Kris Kristofferson." "Yes," he replied, "your cousin told me he had an elderly relative here in Nashville." So *I* turned out to be the "elderly relative" . . . ha . . . ha . . . Kris never did get over that!'

In about 1974 the multi-talented Marijohn moved into a new field – the Gospel Music Field. This was the result, she affirmed of God finding her again! Her classic song 'I have returned' is her personal testimony.

She grew up in a very religious home where her father was the local church deacon and choir leader. At the very slight age of five years she was singing for church activities all over Texas. It became a way of life like eating, sleeping or breathing. She had no spiritual depth at all.

Later her musical interest led her to study music at College where she excelled. She graduated as a school teacher of music because her second love was children. The prospect of a career in the Music Industry, however, excited her far more and she came to Music City USA in 1955. Success followed but somewhere along the ladder in her climb to stardom she became indifferent to God.

'I didn't find God again – he reached down and grabbed me by the hair of the head and said, "You have goofed long enough and that's all there is to it!"'

In 1974 her re-affirmed faith was attractively summarized in her beautiful first gospel album 'I have returned'. Kris Kristofferson, by then a superstar, was only too pleased to write the sleeve notes.

'Kris and Rita happened to be in Nashville recording another album and I was anxious to let them hear what I'd done. I wanted Kris' blessing as he had become the epitomy of country and pop song writing. He came out to Johnny Cash's studios and listened while I remixed my album. One of the songs on the album was "One day at a time" which I had started and Kris helped me to finish. It was gonna be a follow up to "Why me Lord". As Kris heard it played back he turned his head away and I could tell he was crying. After it was all over he looked at me and said, "I wanna tell you I was afraid that you had contrived a bunch of Gospel Songs but after hearing it I got to admit that it's so totally honest." Later he went home to California and sent the liner notes to me and when I read them I cried. We all cry! Yes, we all cry! I guess we're an emotional bunch!'

'I'm really excited about the album,' Marijohn recalls excitedly, 'I used some young voices from the University of Tennessee ... As an ex-schoolteacher I love working with young people ... We'd brought them over from Knoxville originally to record a medley of Kristofferson material on one side of an album and on the other what they do in concert. Kris and I donated our royalties to the University of Tennessee for scholarships. I then told them I'd love to have them work for me. So they got six of them (three girls and three boys) and I rehearsed them with one professional male and one professional female making eight voices. Then I stacked them, which means I over-dubbed them to make sixteen voices. The result was a beautiful, youthful sound.

Not content with writing the songs, singing the songs, rehearsing the choir and musicians, and being the producer she *also* wheeled her piano, from home, down to the studio and played the piano on the album too!

An unusual but interesting song on the album is 'God

is Love' which Marijohn explained in this way. 'This is really my sermon to the preachers (or ministers as you call them in England). I'd gone to the University of Vanderbelt to hear a well-known preacher; I won't say his name, but he's written a couple of popular books. He took his text on exorcism that night and had all the kids scared to death! When I was walking out the door my friend said, "He talked more about the Devil than he did about Jesus!" And it was like a whole bunch of electric light bulbs started going on in my brain. And that's how the song came and the punchline is 'If you're gonna shout about the Devil – give Jesus equal time and remember God is Love!'

Marijohn strongly states, 'To me religion is practical. It's not just a new hat you put on and go to Church on Sunday morning with. You live it every day! It's not only for this world but it's a means of getting to the next one. I hope people can hear the spiritual value in my songs because it seems each new lyric comes out now as a sermonette. And that's the way it's supposed to be!'

Epilogue

As the intangible factors of insecurity and frustration increase and become part of the realities of life in this Western Society of the late 1970's, so too, obviously there will be an increase in demand from the public for songs of inspiration, faith and cheer. Heading this demand will be the plea for the straightforward, uncomplicated, down-to-earth kind of faith that Country Gospel promotes. As George Hamilton IV aptly commented, 'Folks have seen so much of the problems recently that they're getting sick and tired of them and are turning to deeper things . . . and I think it's a good thing.'

One of the artistes who has turned to deeper things and experienced New Life is Wanda Jackson and her husband Wendell Goodman. She recalls, 'God in His Mercy, had allowed us to have practically everything this world could offer. We had a very good marriage, two beautiful children (whom we were not raising properly), making big money, had influential friends, travelled throughout the World; also we had the national and international fame that popular recordings, television shows, and extensive travel brings. Yet . . . with all of these things . . . 'Things' that most people dream of, Wendell and I were not truly happy . . . We felt an incompleteness in our individual lives, and also in our marriage . . . Life held no true meaning or purpose outside of a day to day existence . . . we had become alcoholics, and had created many problems for ourselves under the influence of liquor . . .'

'Then someone cared enough for us to tell us that, regardless of who we were, or what we had, to ever know *the abundant life*, we needed Christ . . . to ever really be happy, we needed Jesus . . . We found what was missing in our lives . . . We didn't have to reform or change in anyway, or give up anything . . . We simply accepted Christ as our Saviour . . .'

'God came into our lives and has given us this joy and peace of mind that we never had . . . He has made our house, a home, has given us a new and real kind of love for each other, for our children, and for other people . . . He has given us a true meaning and purpose for our lives . . . Now we can truly say that we have the abundant life that money and things cannot buy . . . We would like you to have it also . . .'

'THERE ARE FOUR SIMPLE STEPS TO SALVATION

1. Realize that you are a sinner,
   The Bible (The Word of God) says:
   'All have sinned and come short of the glory of God.' (Romans 3:23)
2. Know that there is a penalty for sin,
   The Bible says:
   'The wages of sin is death, but the gift of God is eternal life through Jesus Christ our Lord.' (Romans 6:23)
3. Believe that Christ died for your sins,
   (Jesus has already paid the penalty of sin by dying on the cross),
   The Bible says:
   'If thou shalt confess with thy mouth the Lord

Jesus, and shalt believe in your heart that God raised Him from the dead . . . thou shalt be saved.' (Romans 10:9)

4. Know that you must repent (turn from your sins), The Bible says:

'. . . except ye repent, ye shall all likewise perish.' (Luke 13:3) You can be *saved* from a life of sin and eternity in hell, you can be *saved* to the *abundant life in Christ*, and eternity with Him in Heaven! By accepting Jesus Christ as personal Lord and Saviour *now*!'

Connie Smith would add this serious note:

'You know when you are a kid you never think about dying. You think you've got plenty of time to get right with God, but the Bible says in 2 Cor 6:2, 'Now is the accepted time, behold now is the day of salvation.' I thank God for His Grace that carried me the 27 years I thought I had plenty of time. I thank Him for His Word that helped me to realize that every day 'good' people die and go to hell, and that only through the blood of Jesus Christ can we ever hope to reach heaven. Don't rest in the false security that you "believe in God" – so does Satan – and he is doomed to hell. You have to have Jesus in your heart to claim the promises of God – not an experience someone told you about or one your mother wanted you to have – but one of your own. The Bible says in 1 John 5:13 that you can *know* you have Eternal Life.'

This New Life (abundant and eternal) experienced by many down through the centuries is available to *all* who diligently by faith request it from God.

If you seriously desire to *experience* and *know* this New Life for yourself then make your desire known to 'Contact for Christ', 1 Sherman Road, Bromley, Kent.

'. . . and what is it that God has said? *That He has given us eternal life, and that life is in His Son.* So whoever has the Son has life; whoever does not have His Son, does not have eternal life.'

(1 John 5 : 11–12)